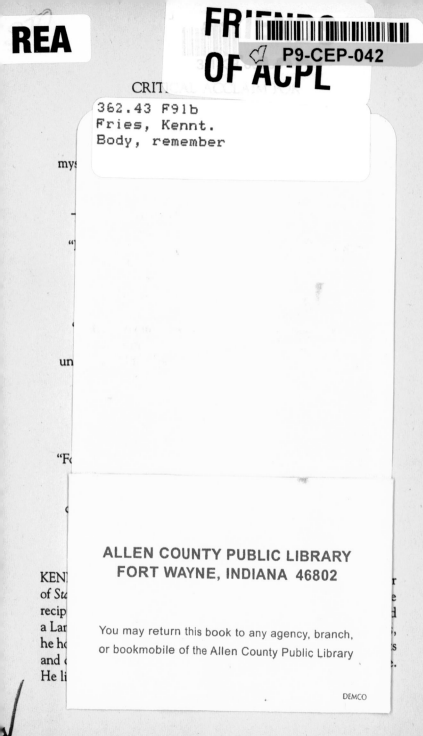

ALSO BY KENNY FRIES

Night After Night
The Healing Notebooks
Anesthesia

Kenny Fries

Body, Remember

A MEMOIR

A PLUME BOOK

AUTHOR'S NOTE
Some of the names of those who appear in this book have been changed to protect the privacy
of those individuals.

PLUME
Published by the Penguin Group
Penguin Putnam Inc., 375 Hudson Street, New York, New York 10014, U.S.A.
Penguin Books Ltd, 27 Wrights Lane, London W8 5TZ, England
Penguin Books Australia Ltd, Ringwood, Victoria, Australia
Penguin Books Canada Ltd, 10 Alcorn Avenue, Toronto, Ontario, Canada M4V 3B2
Penguin Books (N.Z.) Ltd, 182–190 Wairau Road, Auckland 10, New Zealand

Penguin Books Ltd, Registered Offices: Harmondsworth, Middlesex, England

Published by Plume, an imprint of Dutton Signet,
a division of Penguin Putnam Inc.
Previously published in a Dutton edition.

First Plume Printing, February, 1998
10 9 8 7 6 5 4 3 2 1

"Body, Remember" from C.P. Cavafy Collected Poems, translated by Edmund Keeley and Philip
   Sherrard. Copyright © 1980 by Princeton University Press. Reprinted by permission of
   Princeton University Press.

Grateful acknowledgment is made for permission to quote from "Double Ode" by Muriel
   Rukeyser, from A Muriel Rukeyser Reader, 1994, W.W. Norton, N.Y., © William L. Rukeyser.

Ⓟ REGISTERED TRADEMARK — MARCA REGISTRADA

The Library of Congress has catalogued the Dutton edition as follows:
Fries, Kenny.
      Body, remember: a memoir / by Kenny Fries.
            p.   cm.
      ISBN 0-525-94162-2 (hc.)
      ISBN 0-452-27671-3 (pbk.)
      1. Fries, Kenny—Biography.   2. Authors, American—20th century—Biography.
   3. Physically handicapped—United States—Biography.   4. Leg—Abnormalities—
   Patients—United States—Biography.   5. Fries, Kenny.   I. Title.
   PS3556.R568Z464   1997
   362.4'3'092—dc20
   [B]   96-26345
                                                                         CIP

Printed in the United States of America

BOOKS ARE AVAILABLE AT QUANTITY DISCOUNTS WHEN USED TO PROMOTE PRODUCTS
OR SERVICES. FOR INFORMATION PLEASE WRITE TO PREMIUM MARKETING DIVISION,
PENGUIN PUTNAM INC., 375 HUDSON STREET, NEW YORK, NY 10014.

*to my parents
and now
for Kevin*

Body, remember not only how much you were loved,
not only the beds you lay on,
but also those desires glowing openly
in eyes that looked at you,
trembling for you in voices—
only some chance obstacle frustrated them.
Now that it's all finally in the past,
it seems almost as if you gave yourself
to those desires too—how they glowed,
remember, in eyes that looked at you,
remember, body, how they trembled for you in those voices.

—C. P. CAVAFY

CONTENTS

Pay attention to what they tell you to forget

—MURIEL RUKEYSER

ONE

Questions of Origin

And, in the act of writing, to feel our own "questions" meeting the world's "questions," to recognize how we are in the world and the world is in us—

—ADRIENNE RICH

*T*HOSE afternoons I did not take the bus and chose to walk home from high school, I would find this boy, maybe ten or eleven years old, sitting on the stoop of the semidetached house where I imagined he lived. Every time I passed, this boy asked: "Why are your legs the way they are?" And I would answer, "I was born that way," never stopping or slowing down.

The next time I walked down that street, there this boy was, sitting on the stoop, and again he asked me his same question. And I gave him my same answer. That was the entirety of our exchange.

Every time I walked down Bay Forty-third Street in Brooklyn shortly after three in the afternoon, that boy and that question would be waiting for me. Never did I think of answering him in any other way. Or not to answer him at all. Nor did I ever stop to talk to him. And never once did it occur to me that I could walk down another street, not see this boy, and evade his question.

∾

"It could have been worse," my mother always said, imparting her belief that it would have been worse if I had been born mentally retarded, to use the word used at that time.

Or, "He could have been a girl," she would say, explaining that if I were a girl I would have had to wear a skirt or a dress and my legs could not be covered up by the pants she conscientiously cut and hemmed, creating ways for them to fit over my casts and pins when I was recovering from surgery, or over the braces I sometimes wore but do not remember wearing.

I have never told my parents how I feel when people gawk at me while I walk down the street. I don't even have to walk for people to stare.

❧

"A freak, a freak, my daughter gave birth to a freak," my mother's mother yelled, running into the hospital just after I was born. Hearing this, my father fainted. The hospital staff thought he had a heart attack. By the time he revived, my mother, who had gone toxic while giving birth to me, was doing fine.

I try to imagine what my parents said when first seeing each other after I was born. I wonder if they even remember.

I was born, four pounds, five ounces, on September 22, 1960, the second son of Donald and Joan Fries, a lower-middle-class Jewish couple in Brooklyn. My father, then a kosher butcher, had just turned twenty-eight; my mother, then a housewife, was twenty-four. They had been married almost five years. My brother, Jeffrey, was almost three and a half years old.

I remember my young parents as the tall dark-haired handsome couple swirling on the dance floor at numerous weddings and bar mitzvahs. My father wears a dark blue suit and a matching tie; my mother wears her flowing black dress with hand-painted yellow flowers down the front and side. It is as if their love for each other, apparent in the bearing of my mother's regal long neck and in my father's beaming eyes and smile, propels them effortlessly across the floor.

We lived in a sixteen-story dusty-rose brick apartment building, one of a group of five built for middle-income families, in the Bath Beach section, between Coney Island and Bay Ridge, in Brooklyn. In the living room of our small two-bedroom apartment overlooking the busy Belt Parkway fifteen floors below, behind the metal door to 15F, our apartment, I play the upright piano, using the attachment so I can reach the pedal with my longer left leg.

As I play, I catch a glimpse of my parents in the large mirror: my father, despite his bad back injured in the navy, carries my mother over the astroturf green living-room carpet to the plastic-covered lemon chiffon sofa, where he plants a kiss on her lips before they settle down to listen to the silly pop tune that I play.

To this day my parents walk down city streets hand in hand as if, after forty years of marriage, they are still newlyweds. When I was young, walking with them down a street, I giddily stood between them and, each holding onto one of my hands, they with firm grasps lifted me up, swung me forward, and gently returned me a step or two ahead of them to the ground, repeating the lift and descent, sometimes for a whole block at a time, until they had no more strength to do so.

My mother kept our apartment, unlike those of many of my friends, immaculately clean, if cluttered with too many family photos and knickknacks on the furniture, generic paintings and needlepoints on the walls. On weekday nights I expectantly waited to hear my father's distinctive toot-toot whistle when, returning home from work, he came out from the elevator, past the incinerator room, down the speckled olive-green hall. Before he knocked, I opened the door for him, kissed him on the lips, and took the evening edition of the *New York Post*, which I knew had the latest sports news, from his hand.

At the time I was born my father was a religious man. In 1957, three years before I was born, my father's father, upon returning home from Rosh Hashanah services, had a fatal heart attack. On the same day of the Hebrew calendar, three years later, I was born. Brought up in an observant Orthodox Jewish home, my father attended synagogue every Friday night and Saturday morning throughout most of the first decade of my life. We celebrated the holy days. My mother kept a kosher home and changed the dishes and silverware each Passover.

These images of my parents remain steadfast in my mind. But now my memory is tempered with the darker knowledge of what I have come to learn, the turbulent emotions, the untold and sometimes violent story of what was happening beneath the love and smiles. It has taken me many years to remember, let alone understand, the events that happened in 15F, behind that metal door.

Only very recently, during a telephone call just before I was about to move back East from San Francisco, my father told me I had been born a month premature. I have no idea why he had waited so long to tell me. I have no idea why I was premature. Nor does anyone know why at birth I was missing the fibula, why there were sharp anterior curves of the tibia, and flexion contractures of the knees, in both my legs. Absent were two toes and posterior calf bands on each foot. There was no scientific name for my birth defect; in medical records it is simply described that "the child at birth had congenital deformities of the lower extremities."

Nor does reading the medical records my father copied for me after Dr. Milgram died in 1989 provide any answers. Even though I sometimes wake up in the middle of the night, reach down and touch my legs, discovering all over again as if for the first time that, yes, I am disabled, I years ago gave up looking for answers to why I was born with a deformed lower body.

At the time of my mother's pregnancy some women were given thalidomide, a sedative that in 1961 was found not only to ease morning sickness but to cause birth defects similar to my own, as well. Many times I have asked my parents directly whether or not my mother had taken the drug. They have always answered no.

There is no mention of thalidomide in my medical records. But there is also no mention of my having been born premature. Actually, there is no direct mention of my being born at all. The first document in the file is a retrospective summation of my medical history and surgical procedures, dated May 3, 1965.

Today, there are no records that remain to show me how my legs looked when I was born. The X rays, along with the Polaroid photos Dr. Milgram took of my legs, were destroyed after he died. All that is left are the vague medical terms on the thin sheets before me. All I know is from what my father has told me: each leg was no bigger than his finger; each leg was twisted like a pretzel; each leg had no arch to separate leg from foot; each leg was dimpled inches above what would have been my ankle.

I can only imagine what my legs once looked like. I can only imagine that the words I now find to describe that infant's legs are accurate, precise. I can only find words to describe how that infant experienced his body, not actually experience it myself. Everything I write is a translation. Everything I write is necessarily from the perspective of a thirty-five-year-old man who now experiences secondhand what that infant experienced then. I feel what that infant felt through a nervous system years older and by now accustomed to a certain amount of physical and emotional pain. There is no other way of retrieval, no other way to remember.

Familiarity can impede recognition. Over time, the body adjusts until, like the Belt Parkway's constant flow of traffic fifteen floors below our apartment, what was once a severe disturbance becomes white noise. When one is accustomed to it, even a screeching car or ambulance siren will not attract attention. Over time, an alarm clock will no longer alert a sleeper that it is time to wake up, unless the alarm markedly increases in volume or, more likely, if the sound changes just enough, enabling the warning to be heeded once more.

I often try to imagine what it is like for a newly born boy to spend his first six weeks in the hospital, the first four weeks in an incubator. How frightening it must have been for a six-month-old baby boy to be anesthetized and go through hours of surgical procedures. For someone that young to spend so much time in a hospital. It is with a mixture of horror and disbelief that I remember that young infant in the incubator, that body on the operating table, was actually me.

❧

It is cloudy and I think our planned night trip to the beach will not be worthwhile. But as Kevin and I make our way from the parking lot, past the closed concession stand and out onto the beach, the clouds are a curtain, rising as it parts. By the time we have spread our large blanket on the sand, the haze has moved beyond the horizon, revealing the star-filled sky.

It is the midsummer night when the meteor showers will be most active. The night when, if it is clear, it will be easiest to see the shooting stars.

When our eyes adjust to the dark we begin to discern other couples who, like us, have left indoor comfort behind, and lie on their backs, open to the elements, awaiting the beginning of the show. Some, farther down, have lit small fires. Triangles of orange flicker down the beach. We listen to the tide, hear other people laughing.

Soon, after Kevin spots the first sudden flash of light, we are laughing, too. Laughing and pointing to the next star, and the next, and the next traveling in an instant the entire arc of the visible sky. Before the mere flash it takes each star to burst across the galaxy, extinguishing itself as it advances, another has begun its momentary flight.

It has always been difficult for me to comprehend how the stars are sending light from so many years ago. That it took four days for the space shuttle's transmissions of Neptune's likeness to reach awaiting eyes on Earth seems to me unfathomable. The speed of light, 186,000 miles per second, has always been as incomprehensible to my mind as the distance between the Earth and the stars.

Tonight, lying on the beach, Kevin's hand in mine, I begin to name the stars. Not the constellations. Even when Kevin points them out to me, even when I say I can see them, the truth is I cannot distinguish the Big Dipper from Orion, one cluster of stars from another.

Instead I call out, "Shirley," the nickname for my friend Cheryl. Kevin calls out, "Marcia," the name of another friend. Soon we are naming every flash of light, using the names of our friends' ex-boyfriends, and when we run out of them we use our own.

"Polio," "spina bifida," "cerebral palsy," I hear myself naming out loud diseases that in another world, a world in which the connotations of disability are not pejorative, would be perfect names for shooting stars.

Tonight, looking at the sky, I know what it is I want to do. I want to be in an open space and feel Kevin's body close to mine as we look around us, sharing what is happening this very moment before our eyes.

But on this clear night I am able not only to understand the clarity, the intimacy both physical and intangible, that two different people can share, but at the same time I can see once again moving from the horizon onto the shore, the haze that only hours ago made it unlikely that we would be able to witness the stars.

Kevin's hand feels cold on my skin. As we watch the sky his

hand mindlessly moves up and down my leg. The second finger on his left hand begins to play with one of the holes adjoining the scar, just above where my right foot juts out at almost ninety degrees from my leg.

Suddenly, involuntarily, I jump.

"What's the matter?" Kevin asks.

I take a deep breath and the warm night air gets caught in my throat. I taste sand and ocean salt. But all I can smell is ether—the antiseptic odor that pervaded Dr. Milgram's crowded waiting room to his hospital office, when I was young.

How do I explain to Kevin the enormous respect I had for my orthopedic surgeon, Dr. Joseph Milgram? How do I describe the people from all over the world who sat with me in that fluorescently lit, linoleum-tiled waiting room? How do I begin to tell him how Dr. Milgram made me feel special?

I always bragged to my friends about the important doctor who took care of me in Manhattan. Even Alice, his secretary, was surprised when Dr. Milgram asked her to write a check to pay for a subscription to the magazine I would always read in the waiting room. He even gave my parents his home telephone number, showed us photos of his upstate farm, and once told my father that he felt like he was my grandfather.

Kevin watches the stars. I want to tell him why I jumped. I want to tell him about the disagreement between Dr. Milgram and the resident doctor. How, in 1970, after the major five-hour reconstructive surgery on my right foot and leg, during which my foot was connected to my leg only by a single blood vessel near where he had been touching, my leg, held in position by two pins, was heavily bandaged but not put in a cast. When the resident made his rounds he put the bandaged leg in a plastic bag. When Dr. Milgram came the next day, he took it off, saying that it needed to breathe. The next day the resident put the bag back on and Dr. Milgram on his next visit took it off. I want to tell Kevin how these two men, supposedly working together so I could walk better, did not agree on the best way to lessen the chance of infection in my leg.

I want to tell Kevin why I jumped when his finger grazed that hole. I want him to know that when the pins were removed Dr. Milgram at first insisted that it could be done without anesthetics. I want to be able to describe the pain when that was tried, how it still racks my body when the holes where the pins were inserted are touched. I want Kevin to know that the next day, when the pins were successfully removed, I was in the operating room under anesthesia. I want to tell him that even though Dr. Milgram did not know what caused my legs to be deformed, I needed to trust him. I want Kevin to know that despite any mistake he, Kevin, might make, something harmful he might say or do, I want to trust him, as I trusted my doctor.

I want to tell Kevin that although I am no longer young, and that I understand more with each passing year, I am still afraid. Afraid that after all these years, after all the surgery, after all the psychotherapy, some wounds can never heal, that some wounds are actually the scars.

An hour later we are driving the short distance back to my house, where only a few weeks ago Kevin came to spend the summer with me. I feel his hand on my neck. Barely over five feet tall, I cannot reach the gas pedal or the brake with my legs, so I use hand controls to drive: a simple metal lever, up and toward me for gas, down and away for brake. My left hand on the controls, my right hand steering, when driving I have little time, except when stopped at a red light or on longer drives when I can hold the hand controls and steady the steering wheel at the same time, to hold my lover's hand. Instead, I push my head back into Kevin's palm.

❧

After I was born, my parents took me from hospital to hospital, from doctor to doctor. My parents did not have much money but they somehow managed to take me to some of the best hospitals in New York City. All the doctors who saw me recommended the same thing: amputation of both my legs.

My parents are not the most worldly couple. Born during the Depression, Jews who lived through World War II, their aspirations were those of security and stability. Though intelligent, my father never graduated from high school; my mother, though witty and inquisitive, always tends to look at the material side of things. I was born in 1960, a time when conformity was much the vogue. Disability rights was not even a nascent movement and most people were not conscious of the concerns of persons with disabilities. My parents never sought out a support group for parents of disabled children. Most disabled children were institutionalized or sent to "special" schools.

When I had my yearly appointments with Dr. Milgram I know my mother was there, but in my memory my father has taken center stage as he positions my legs for the X-ray technicians, replasters my casts, bathes me.

My mother was at my bedside every single hour of visiting hours every time I was in the hospital. It was my mother who brought everything I asked for to the hospital. It was my mother who sat on hall patrol so I could be mainstreamed, attending regular kindergarten after I had surgery in 1966. It was my mother with whom I would sit and laugh as she recited Mark Antony's funeral oration speech from *Julius Caesar*, the only high school Shakespeare she remembers, while she cooked me an early dinner so I could go off to rehearse plays when I was in high school, and who would pick me up later that night when rehearsals were over. But in my memory, my mother is, curiously, emotionally absent. I know where she was, but until very recently I did not know what she felt.

How do I begin to imagine what my young mother felt giving birth to a disabled son? What did my mother feel as she looked at me in an incubator that provided the warmth I needed to survive? If it has been difficult for me to uncover, identify, and understand much of what I experienced, it must be just as, if not more, difficult for my mother to do so. I have lived my entire life wondering what might tip the balance and cause my mother to lose control, unraveling the potent mixture of love and guilt, anger, fear, and shame—all her emotions I cannot describe—that has knotted my mother and me together more tightly than the umbilical cord from which I was long ago set free.

∾

With the development of amniocentesis and ultrasound techniques, parents are now put into a situation with which my parents were not confronted when I was born in 1960. It is now possible for parents to know at various stages during pregnancy whether or not their child will be born deformed. In the case of amniocentesis any genetic defects can be detected quite early in a pregnancy. Ultrasound can detect nongenetic deformities much later on. Knowing this information, some parents may now choose to abort their unborn disabled child. Did my parents ever wish I hadn't been born?

I now live precariously with the knowledge that today, because my parents could know I would be deformed, they might decide to not allow me to be born. I know how dispensable my life and the lives of so many disabled people have been in many societies, most notably Germany under Nazi rule. I am intimate with the mystery that if I was born in a different time, at a different place, or even to different parents in the same time and place, I might not have had this life to write about at all.

It seems that to my twenty-something parents, my mother and my father in 1960, amputation would have been the logical solution to what was then perceived as their "problem."

Amputation would, in many ways, get rid of the problem. At the very least it would minimize the risks, both emotional and financial. And if the doctors said this would be best, why not?

But my parents did not agree to allow any doctor to amputate my legs. My father was told by a rabbi about a Dr. Joseph Milgram. He and my mother asked my pediatrician, Dr. Armand Moss, what he knew about this Dr. Milgram. Dr. Moss looked him up in a physician's reference and told my parents: "He's one with Macy's prices."

Undaunted, my parents got an appointment with the important doctor, chief of orthopedic surgery at the Hospital for Joint Diseases on 125th Street and Madison Avenue in New York City. At the time of my first appointment, Dr. Milgram was already sixty years old and one of the most highly regarded orthopedic surgeons in New York, a doctor's doctor who was constantly asked for advice by leading physicians around the world. When Dr. Milgram married his wife he told her that the only way she could understand him was to become a doctor herself. She, as well as his two sons, became doctors.

When I asked my father why he decided to heed Dr. Milgram and not the countless other doctors to whom I had been taken, he said he didn't decide, Dr. Milgram just started telling him what he was going to do. "Come here, Father, come here, Mother," the bespectacled Dr. Milgram, dressed in a rumpled white shirt, black bow tie, and slightly worn, slightly oversize tweed pants held up by suspenders, said as he began to announce out loud his plans for their child. In his brusque, somewhat nasal voice he impatiently barked orders to Alice, his secretary—"Haven't you gotten me radiology on the line?"—while he read to my parents what he was writing, illegibly, in their son's medical records.

Through their perseverance and driven by a belief in what I still do not know, my parents had found this unduly dedicated if always-in-a-hurry, seemingly distracted, slightly disheveled man whose fascination with clocks gave him an imaginative understanding of the structure and movement of human bones unsurpassed for his time. It was this short, portly cross between a mad professor and a bookish farmer, this doctor who walked like a duck, who would be responsible for the reconstruction of my legs.

"I would be positive this boy will eventually walk with straight legs," Dr. Milgram writes in my records, "because he has the feet capable of coming up to right angles." When I wake up during the night and make my way to the bathroom, I think about how during that first visit Dr. Milgram told my parents he wanted me, when I was old enough, to be able to get up and get myself a drink of water in the middle of the night, and when doing so to feel my own legs touch the floor.

Dr. Milgram promised my parents that by age eighteen I would live a normal life. He was way off the mark. My life was pretty normal—at least that's what it looked like from the outside—very early on.

❧

I have three toes on each foot. My medical records state that the biggest toe on each foot is a lateral toe; and even though these toes are covered with a single nail they are probably conjoined toes because they are twice as large as each second toe. To me, this toe is simply my big toe just like everybody else's big toe.

When I was a little boy I waited for my big toe on each foot to give birth to two more toes so I would then have, like everybody else, the normal five. I assumed that this was how everyone obtained five toes, by a process like a paramecium's mitosis.

This childhood myth made me feel more like other little boys. This fanciful explanation enabled me to make a place in

my own mind where it was okay to have this physical difference, at least for a while.

I am told how for the first few years there was doubt I would
ever be able to move by myself, let alone walk. But one day
when my great aunt Bea was preparing to bathe me in the sink,
I began to crawl. She screamed out to my parents, who were in
the next room.

Wearing feet pajamas, I would, legs encasted, move around
the house in a baby's walker. I was an active boy, often pulling
off my casts between the bars of my crib. Loosened, the casts
would slip down my leg into the feet of the pajamas, making it
seem as if my legs had suddenly lengthened.

I am always told the story of how I learned to walk while
wearing a cast on each leg. The casts had walkers at the
bottom, my parents would tell me, as if that made the story
easier to fathom.

Throughout my early records, two medical terms are prominent: *valgus*, which means knock-kneed; and *equinus*, alluding
to horses' hooves, meaning my feet were like closed fists.

An entry states that on July 1, 1963, despite my brace
causing pressure symptoms around my right calf, Dr. Milgram
recommended I remain in braces during the summer, in plaster
casts during the winter. Almost a year later, on June 17, 1964,
Dr. Milgram writes: "Patient to keep leg brace on with knee
locked progressively in extension to overcome flexion contracture. Right brace readjusted. Daily exercises and continued
brace adjustment prescribed to hold right heel down and bring
about gradual improvement."

Reading these records it is difficult to believe I could have
learned to walk in two casts. It is as if Dr. Milgram speaks for
me when he writes that "the present X ray, taken by holding
the foot, cannot possibly reveal the true state of affairs."

But I never doubted my parents' rendition of my learning to
walk until much later. It dovetailed perfectly with the image

my parents had popularized, that I was a "superboy," the image of myself I wanted to believe.

I always hear about all the things I was able to do as a child. No one ever tells me about any difficulty, physical or emotional, that I encountered as a boy. And until I was in college I do not remember, not even once, talking with somebody about any difficulty that I was experiencing and could not handle alone.

By September 15, 1965, the records state that my left leg was one inch longer than the right leg and that I was not growing very rapidly at the time. Dr. Milgram was concerned about my knees, and elastic pressure, attached to the upright of the brace, was used to keep them straight. Measurements list my right leg extended to 160 degrees, the left to 165.

The end of this entry says that although I should wear my braces in school, I was able to run around outside of my braces, and that I should be frequently permitted to do so.

I would not understand how difficult it must have been for me to learn to walk until 1970. Recovering from surgery, I used a wheelchair as I healed. After I had the surgical pins from my right leg removed, I was too afraid to put my foot down, fearing it would not be strong enough to bear my weight. No matter how hard he tried, Dr. Milgram could not get me to put my leg down. We must have been in his office close to an hour as I stubbornly refused to even touch my toe to the uncarpeted floor.

I still see Dr. Milgram, sixty-nine years old at the time, his gray cowlick plastered to his forehead. The beads of sweat on his silver mustache remain magnified in my mind. I still hear the insistent buzz of the fluorescent light above. My body still contorts from the fear and the built-up frustration leading to the eventual triumph when I finally trusted enough to allow my foot to touch the tile floor, the relief that once again my right leg would not shatter from the weight it used to so easily bear.

❧

I carry my father's tennis racquet to the handball court across the lawn from the two-room bungalow my family rents each summer at Lansman's in Woodbourne, New York. I bounce the tennis ball and begin to volley against the wall. I chase after the ball and even if it bounces twice, or three times, I hit it back against the wall. Having yet to learn to hit a backhand, I try to maneuver so I can hit the ball with my forehand. I attempt to learn a two-fisted backhand like Chris Evert used when I watched her at the U.S. Open on TV.

Needing a rest I sit down, the racquet balancing on my crossed legs, the ball on top of the racquet. The midafternoon sun in late July is strong and from the pool nearby I can hear kids shouting, splashing when they dive into the water. When I loosen up, turning my body from side to side, I notice my father standing on the bungalow porch. Even from this distance I can feel him watching me.

I get up and begin to hit the ball against the wall again. This time I try to hit it harder. And harder. After reaching the ball on a single bounce a few times I hit the ball with too much force and it ricochets off the wall much too quickly and skips by me, bouncing off the court and rolling down the hill almost halfway to the bungalow, where I know my father stands watching.

When I bend down to retrieve the ball I see my father watching me. I do not want him to know I see him, so after I pick it up I quickly pirouette and return to the court. After a successful volley hitting it back a dozen times I run with my racquet past my father into the bungalow, just in time to change into my bathing suit and get to the pool before closing.

When I get to the pool most parents and their children have left for the day. I throw my towel on a wood lounge chair and walk methodically into the pool one step at a time, slowly getting used to the chilly water in the shallow end. When I finally turn around to dunk myself in the water and begin to swim, I see my father on his way from the bungalow to the pool.

❧

I am not yet five, shopping with my mother under the el on Eighty-sixth Street when I yell, "Look at the midget!" when a midget passes by.

Often, young children will gleefully point at me and say the same thing I said years ago on Eighty-sixth Street. "Why do they call me midget?" I ask my mother.

"They don't know any better," she answers.

"Midget" was one of the epithets with which my older brother, Jeffrey, would taunt me. I never asked my mother why my brother called me midget or if she ever told him not to say it. But why did *I* say it out loud on Eight-sixth Street? Had I learned this word from my brother? Did he learn it when other kids embarrassed me in the street? How did he feel when they called me names?

Later, when I was in elementary school, there was a midget named Scott who was a grade or two ahead of me. After seeing Scott and being called again and again a midget by my brother, I asked my mother: "Am I a midget?"

"No, you're not a midget," she told me.

"What's the difference between me and a midget?"

"A midget needs clothes specially ordered for him," was my mother's answer. "You don't need special clothes."

Scott was the only other student who was what we now would call physically different in the schools I attended. Even after I graduated on to junior high school I would meet people whom I vaguely recognized from elementary school who would call me Scott. I never corrected them.

I never spoke to Scott, never got to know him beyond the fact that I knew his clothing had to be specially ordered to fit him. I was scared to be near him, didn't want anyone to ever see me talking to him. My heart raced when I saw him precede me down the hall.

Now, although I still feel oddly ashamed about having to do so, I find tailors who will cut and hem my pants so they will fit me. Now, I know that Scott and I had more in common than my mother told me. Now, I wonder if anyone ever thought that Scott was me.

∾

I told my parents I was going to be a basketball player for UCLA. I brought books like *Strange but True Basketball Stories* to read in the waiting room on my visits to Dr. Milgram and he would gruffly ask why I wanted to be a basketball player. "All they have are sweaty armpits," he told me. "What about being a doctor?" he asked.

Before everyone grew much taller than I, despite the discrepancy in my leg lengths, despite the problems with my knees, despite my lack of external hip rotation, before my physical disability became an obvious disadvantage, I played sports with my friends.

By the time I reached the end of elementary school, I gave up playing, coaching my sixth-grade class team in an intramural basketball league. But I didn't give up sports completely. In ninth grade I won an award for hanging on the parallel bars longer than anyone else in the school. Even at that age, I gravitated to what I could do, and with a great deal of effort I did it well.

But soon I stopped having anything to do with playing sports in public with my friends. During the summer, using my allergies as an excuse, I would stay inside reading when my friends went out to play.

But my interest in following sports grew in intensity as I realized I no longer could successfully compete with my peers. I became obsessed with statistics, copying down the league standings, as well as the individual leaders, week after week during each season.

I picked up my intense interest in watching and following sports by myself. My father and brother to this day have no interest in sports. I have been a sports fan since 1969, when the New York Mets overcame all odds by winning the World Series.

That week in October 1969, when the weekday World Series games were still played during the afternoon, I rushed home from the school bus so I would not miss the game on television. Later, the next spring, the New York Knicks won the NBA championship and I was hooked even more. I was transfixed when during the seventh and deciding game, the Knicks' center, Willis Reed, defying his injured knee, came onto the court, inspiring his teammates to victory.

I created an imaginary basketball-like league, a league with its own detailed history comprised of made-up players, statistics, and awards. I kept notebooks filled with these imagined facts about these fantasy players and teams. My preferred team I named the New York Athletics. My preferred player was Kenny Yex, pronounced "X," who was seven feet, eleven inches tall. He was the best player who ever lived.

I set up a small wastebasket on the living-room sofa, drew court lines in the astroturf-like green carpet, and ran back and forth with a tennis ball, attempting to shoot the ball into the wastebasket. Placed on the couch it was not very high, enabling me to perform athletic feats like shooting a hook shot straight down into the basket, or slam-dunking, easily. I announced the game out loud to myself, being all players on both teams, all at the same time.

"Ladies and gentlemen, playing center for the world champion New York Athletics," I announced in a voice imitated from the familiar Madison Square Garden announcer I knew from the radio. "Shoots and scores," I told my invisible audience, as I caught my breath from running the short length back and forth across the living-room carpet.

 ❧

When I was young, I performed: I sang, played the piano, acted in plays and musicals.

But by the time I reached high school, something began to change. One afternoon, coming home from school, as I reached for my keys, I noticed the reflection of the full-length of my body in our apartment building's glass front doors. To my surprise, the reflection that confronted me in the glass was not the image of myself I saw in my mind. Did what I see reflected back to me correspond to how others perceived me?

For months, I could not get rid of this image: my asymetrical body lurching forward with each step. Although I never told anybody, I became self-conscious, felt my deformity was too obvious, drew too much attention. Disabled, I felt everybody's eyes—like the boy who asked me about my legs, the kids who would call me midget—were transfixed on my legs. What was I doing on stage? I felt like a fraud.

Who would cast me in the parts I wanted to play? And when I wouldn't get a part I wanted I was never sure whether it was because of my lack of talent, or because of my physical difference. I was unbalanced by these doubts.

I still have dreams in which during a performance I cannot remember my lines and have to ad-lib as I go along. In other dreams I know my lines but have lost my voice. I try to continue until I realize nobody can hear me.

Now I understand that as a teenager I intuitively knew being an actor with a physical disability would be limiting. I was unconsciously learning what my disability might prevent me from doing. I was also experiencing loss. But even though being unaware leaves no opportunity to grieve, the transition from acting to directing, like my earlier transition from sports participant to spectator, eased what might have been an otherwise unbearable sense of isolation.

Nevertheless, I fell in love with theater, and in lieu of high school English courses, I became a member of my high school repertory company. I gave up acting and began to direct, eventually well enough to direct the company's full-length production during my senior year.

ॐ

"He wanted to be a basketball player at UCLA," Helen, the daughter of my parents' best friends, Charlotte and Sam, who lived down the hall, tells Kevin. Eight years older than I, it was Helen to whom, as I grew older, I would confide. It was this five-foot bundle of Brooklyn Jewish energy, with cropped dark hair and whose face, even after cosmetic surgery, is dominated by a prominent nose, with whom I discussed books and films, as well as the plays I directed in school.

It was Helen who first told me how handsome I was, making me for the first time conscious of how unattractive I felt. In math class I could see Helen's fifteenth-story window, and if she was home she would raise and lower the bright red shade so I'd know she was thinking of me.

"Anything he did—dancing, singing, tumbling around—his parents watched him do it and we all applauded. Anything he wanted to do, we believed he could do it," she tells Kevin.

"But who could believe a disabled child could be a basketball player?" I want to say. "They didn't believe I could be a basketball player." Or maybe they did. Did they actually believe that I was the "superboy" that they still talk about today? Did my parents succumb, as I did, to the still prevalent myth that disabled people could overcome their disabilities, could succeed at anything, if they just tried hard enough? Despite not having use of his legs due to polio, FDR became president, after all.

The flip side of such blanket encouragement is pity, I think, as Helen and Kevin continue to get acquainted. But pity is not something I usually associate with my parents' attitude toward me. It is partly how my paternal grandmother felt about me, combined with her begrudging Old World respect and love. When I was born her first response was to cry.

Somewhere inside the small child I then was I must have known that my fantasy of being a basketball player was, in reality, impossible. What about the things that were in my reach? If my parents believed I could be a basketball player, how seriously could I take their belief that I could achieve my realistic aspirations? If I interrupted Helen's conversation with Kevin and asked her if she actually believed I could do anything I wanted to do, what would she answer?

∽

I know my past by knowing my scars. Where once a surgeon tore my skin and entered my body for reconstruction, or removal, now these scars have become the points of entry into my past, into those places where, as a child, I was unable to go safely. In this way my scars do not exist only on my skin, but remain inscribed on the cortex of my brain, the section where memory is stored.

My medical records state that between February 8, 1961, when I first was taken to Dr. Milgram, and December 11, 1964, when this particular medical summary ends, I was admitted into the hospital for three operations. Two took place in 1961, one on my left leg on March 14, one on my right leg on April 20. The third surgery was performed on my right leg on February 11, 1964.

"We must overcome foot before work with knee flexion," Dr. Milgram notes in these early medical records. His desire to increase the angle of my ankle, as well as the extension of my leg, were achieved by these three operations, in which Dr. Milgram excised a fibrous band, and lengthened the Achilles tendon first on my left, then on my right leg. The third procedure further lengthened the Achilles tendon on my right leg. Between surgeries my legs remained in casts.

As an infant I was brought to the hospital and then discharged the next day, unable to have surgery because I had developed a fever. The medical records show that this happened twice before the first surgery in 1961, and once before the second to be performed that same year.

The doctors assumed that I was allergic to one of the pre-anesthetics routinely administered the night before surgery. They never thought my having a fever before surgery was my body's apt response to the anxiety and fear of a six-month-old infant.

According to these records, casts on both legs had to be changed numerous times. For these years there are fifty-five entries, which includes all visits to Dr. Milgram or the hospital, for surgery, cast changes, or routine office calls. By 1964 this early reconstruction of my lower legs and feet reached a conclusion, and I was fitted for braces to lock my knees in order to overcome the flexion contracture at those vital joints.

The physical remains from these three early surgeries can still be easily discerned on my skin. On the outer side of my left leg there is a scar running six inches long between my foot and my knee, and a shorter one in almost the same place on my right leg. Close to the scar on my right leg is another scar, thinner but just as long.

I have no physical or emotional recollection of these three operations. However, when I touch these scars, or when they are touched by someone else, a sensation travels from the base of my spine all the way up to the base of my neck. If I touch these scars long enough my body will begin to shudder, as if my skin needs to escape from a prolonged shock of electricity, as if the sensation is trying to find a quick exit, my body a release from an uncomfortable surge.

There are two other scars on my right leg, remains from surgery on February 2, 1966, and June 18, 1970. The scar from 1966 runs up the side of my right leg beginning at the knee. It is approximately four inches long, ending just below my outer thigh. At the base of this scar is a slight indentation from where a pin was inserted during surgery to hold the knee in place.

The other scar on my right leg is just above where my foot meets my leg, close to where my ankle would be if I had one. The scar itself is quite thin and runs almost six inches in length. On either side of this scar, on each side of my leg, are four holes, two on each side, where two pins were inserted to keep the reconstructed bones in place while healing.

Attached to these two later scars on my right leg are memories. Over time, like the scars themselves, these stories have stretched larger, becoming permanent permutations of my psyche, just as the scars have become permanent markings on my skin. And like all scars, these memories, along with the emotions that swell up along with them, grow older and alter with time. At different times different parts are highlighted, while other parts simply fade.

ॐ

When I take a bath I lock the bathroom door. Sometimes, I bathe myself for close to an hour so when I am finished my skin, though white and wrinkled, seems transparent. When I was young, taking a bath I discovered that water magnifies sound. If I submerged my head under water and listened, I was able to hear people moving in the apartment below. Under water, I was able to hear my parents' voices, though not what they were saying, in other rooms.

During my first year in high school, after a bath I noticed something glistening at the base of the scar on the side of my right leg. I squeezed the area, as you would a pimple, and out of the scar and onto my finger came a tiny sliver of silver metal. I was not sure what it was but I thought it a remnant of the pin inserted during the surgery when I was six years old.

This surgery, a major procedure called a torsion osteotomy, was supposed to rotate my right knee to face forward. Although in the years since this surgery was performed it has never been openly discussed, I have always known that this surgery was not successful. After the surgery, when I was put in a very large cast that covered my entire right leg up past my hips to my stomach, I asked why the cast was so big. I felt confined. I was told it was done because after my last operation I was too wild.

Holding that small piece of silver metal in my hand, I remembered that night, perhaps a few weeks or a month after I had returned from the hospital, when I got myself out of bed and dragged myself into my parents' room while holding in my hand the metal pin that I had dislodged from my right leg.

No matter how hard I stared at the silver sliver, still wet and glistening in my hand, I could not remember what happened next. Nor could I remember my parents' reaction. What did we do with the pin? Why was it so easily dislodged?

According to my medical records Dr. Milgram planned to perform this surgery with the help of his assistant, Dr. Victor Frankel. Dr. Frankel, thirty years younger than Dr. Milgram, still wears large owlish glasses the size of his forced smile. Unlike Dr. Milgram, he would always wear his white doctor's garb. Tall and broad-shouldered, he physically towered over the portly Dr. Milgram, but Dr. Frankel, only in his mid-thirties at the time, did not possess his boss's self-confidence or Old World charm. He seemed decidedly uncomfortable at having to exist in the shadow of Dr. Milgram's ever active mind, and never engendered the trust Dr. Milgram inspired.

The morning of the surgery I did not see Dr. Milgram in the operating room; Dr. Frankel performed the surgery without him. I remember telling my parents that Dr. Milgram wasn't there. I remember their silence. Did my parents believe what I was telling them?

My father blamed my taking the pin from my leg as the cause of that surgery's failure. What did he think when I called him into the bathroom to show him what I had found?

Years later, in my medical file I find a note written after an examination on April 6, 1966. The note says that when the sutures from the surgery were removed an area of proud flesh, caused by the formation of small protuberances on the surface of a wound that is healing, was excised and treated with a tincture of silver nitrate. Could it be silver nitrate that I found, years after surgery, lodged in my skin? In these same records I also discover that no one told me that the large confining cast had been used not as a punishment because I was wild but to limit the rotation of my body.

❧

There is one other scar that has become part of this physical and emotional constellation. This short two-inch scar is on my left hand, where a tumor began to grow on the metacarpal during my junior year in high school, when I was sixteen.

My left thumb, as well as the web between my thumb and second finger, began to swell. The area became slightly red, felt warm, was tender. When I told my parents they at first did not think much of it, the same reaction they had ten years earlier in 1966, when, after a long day of shopping, we were on the way into our apartment building when an out-of-control bicyclist collided with my left leg, which dangled out of my stroller.

I immediately knew my leg was broken, but my parents did not believe me that first night when I was in excruciating pain and could not put my foot down. This accident happened shortly after my recuperation from major surgery on my right leg, and my wearied parents could not bring themselves to admit that something could now be wrong with my stronger left leg. After months of my difficult recuperation, the random act of a bicyclist stretched the limit of what my parents could endure.

That night of the bicycle accident, despite the pain, and although I knew something was very wrong, I entertained myself with the liquid bubble-maker bought for me earlier in the day. But in the morning, I was still in pain. I was still unable to put my foot down. My parents called Dr. Milgram, and meeting us in the emergency room at the hospital, he confirmed my diagnosis of a broken leg.

Eventually, although aspirin seemed to provide some relief for the pain in my left hand, I could no longer move my thumb, nor use my left hand. I was kept awake at night by my frantic thoughts of the unknown organism growing in my hand. I would doze off only to be startled by my dream of an alien being taking over my body. Looking at my thumb, I believed I could see something alive moving underneath my skin. Was it cancer? I began to imagine what my life would be like with an amputated left hand.

When my hand continued to swell, my parents took me to see our family doctor, who put my hand in a splint so it could not move. Later that week, in an X ray, he found a growth the size of a dime.

My father called Dr. Milgram to set up an appointment so

he could take a look at my hand. Dr. Milgram was by then seventy-six years old and was no longer performing surgery. He recommended that his successor as director of orthopedics at the Hospital for Joint Diseases, Dr. Harold Robbins, take a look, and perform the necessary surgery.

Fortunately, the previous year there had been X rays taken of both hands when Dr. Milgram wanted to check on growth plates to see if I had stopped growing. The X rays of the previous year showed no sign of any tumor in any part of my left hand. Dr. Milgram allayed our fears that the tumor was in any way related to the birth defects of my legs. Until then, that question lurked in the back of our minds.

I would not go in for the surgery on my hand without Dr. Milgram being there. At my request, and with my parents willing to pay for his time, he agreed to supervise the surgery, a situation that did not please Dr. Robbins, whom I did not like and with whom I did not get along. But Dr. Milgram thought him the best man for the job, and with my trusted doctor in charge, I agreed that this necessary surgery be done.

∾

In 1976, when I enter the Hospital for Joint Diseases, I pass the familiar formal portrait of a younger Dr. Milgram, in a dark suit looking like a bank president, flanked by portraits of his predecessors. Only his customary bow tie, the slightest twinkle in his eye, personalizes an otherwise forbidding depiction.

When I enter the hospital there are no semiprivate rooms available, and even though I am sixteen years old I am given a bed in the same children's ward in which I have been placed all those other times I have been in the hospital.

I have never forgotten this ward. The always open door to the ward is part of a half wall; the upper half is glass, allowing nurses and passersby in the hallway to peer in at will.

One nurse, still on staff since I was born, remembers me. This is a big deal, is comforting, to my parents, but reminds me of having been in this ward when I was a child. But now, I am old enough to better understand the seriousness of what is going on. I do not want to be treated as if I am still that young, helpless child.

Although it has been ten years since I've been in this room, it has haunted me for years. There are sixteen beds, eight to a wall. Of all the patients with whom I shared this ward, for a week or two or maybe for just a few days, never to see or hear from them again when they left the hospital, I remember only one boy.

The night before my surgery in 1970, my parents remained with me until the nurse came in to tell them they must, like everyone else, go home. As they waited by the elevator I saw my parents through the windowed wall and was overtaken by an unexplainable panic that once the elevator came and its door closed I would never see my mother or my father again. I started to scream out loud, but no nurse rushed in to see what was wrong.

Then, I realized the small boy, even younger than I, had made his way from his bed directly across the ward to mine. Perched by my shoulder, sitting on the upper edge of my bed, he petted me and from the corner of my eye I saw his small webbed hand, all five fingers stuck together, stroking my head. He played with my hair as he whispered in my ear.

I hear the creak of the rarely drawn hospital curtains, the only partition between patients, scraping on their rusty tracks. The blue plastic institutional chairs with metal legs, at each bedside, are the same chairs in which my parents sat, day after day, during my previous hospital stays. The one television, high up on a shelf no patient could reach, is still at the end of the ward. For years I have wondered what the view might be outside the window, which I still cannot reach.

When I enter the hospital and am put in this familiar ward I am terrified. It is as if all the fear stored up from all my previous surgeries and hospital stays, after years of inattention, has risen from where I was sure it had until now been buried.

A nurse arrives to take my blood soon after I settle in. The needle in my arm, I faint. I have never fainted when having blood drawn before. Never before have I even felt light-headed or dizzy.

While I am blacked out the surgery takes place in my mind. When I revive, thinking the surgery has already been performed, I am very disappointed to find out that I fainted just a minute before, that the surgery will take place tomorrow, that nothing has yet transpired.

When I wake up in the middle of the night I hear sounds I know are not happening now, but happened long ago in this same hospital ward. I remember the last time I was here, how the night before surgery, after all the preparation was done and I was no longer allowed to eat any food or drink any liquid, I was put in the small room next to the children's ward, where I was supposed to sleep alone.

All night I heard an older woman screaming directly across the hall. The nurse went to quiet her down and no sooner was she gone than the woman began screaming again. Eventually, this woman's screams were ignored. The sound from the room across the hall seemed to get closer and closer, get deeper and deeper, as if the sounds began to emanate not from her throat, not from her gut, but from my own.

If I sleep tonight it will be a fitful sleep, not knowing whether I am awake or sleeping. I cannot escape those screams which, along with the anguish, work themselves into my dreams.

❧

Once inside the institution you no longer control your body. The smells of ether and alcohol blend with the odors of ammonia and cafeteria food. The distinctness of your own breath, your own sweat, is replaced by what permeates each hospital room and hall. After only a few hours it is as if these smells emanate from your own body, as well.

The nondescript starkness of the walls and furnishings, the lighting—all that white—makes the experience surreal. Everybody is dressed the same. Disembodied voices and signals you do not understand are heard over the announcement system.

You must place your trust in men and women, often overworked and in pressured situations, who need to look at your clear plastic hospital bracelet or at your medical chart to know who you are. You are known to the staff by your medical problem, defined by what you have come to them to cure. You encounter in your semiprivate room, or in my case a ward, other patients with various medical problems and various modes of coping, or not. You are forced to share the most intimate moments in front of all these people you have never met before.

During a hospital stay I am often visited by interns on their morning rounds. A group of five or ten, led by an older doctor, appear, usually in midmorning, and interrupt whatever I am doing. Not bothering to draw the curtain around my bed, one doctor pulls up my bedsheets and, even though not related to my current medical problem, the interns gawk at my legs. Behind their clipboards and frozen stares, the interns cannot hide their astonishment when the doctor tells them, "He walks. And he plays basketball."

As the doctors talk behind their clipboards they know nothing about me but what I can and can't do with my legs. I just lie there, smiling. Without asking permission to do so, they use my body as an example of what miracles the masters of medical science can perform. But as I seem to dutifully comply, the clipboard-wielding doctors do not know that when they look at my body I am not only damaged, broken, unwhole, but also Kenny Yex, seven-feet eleven in my mind.

❧

The night before surgery, I eat my last meal and drink my last swallow of water, the last thing I will taste until hours after the surgery is over. After my parents have been asked to leave, an orderly comes to clean and shave the area near where the surgery is to take place. If I protest I know I will be told the removal of body hair is necessary for sterilization, to reduce the risk of infection, so nothing will get in the doctor's way.

The curtain is drawn around my bed. I fix my eyes on the shadows of fellow patients who I know must be trying to peer in through the not fully closed partition. As the orderly prepares me for surgery I hold still—"One slight move and you wouldn't be happy with the results," the orderly tells me through his laughter. I hold my breath, as I have done for so many X-ray technicians, breathing out only when I hear the razor dunked in the bowl of water. I want to peer over the bowl's edge to see what the razor has skimmed off, but I am afraid to make even the smallest movement.

Finished, with one quick motion the orderly slides the curtain open—no one there, after all. He carries the bowl and razor to the sink and runs the water, dumping all that he has taken from me, before he waves good-bye.

The next morning, soon after I am wakened by the nurse's arrival to take my temperature, I am given a preanesthetic that within the next half hour will dry me out, make me groggy. I am dressed in a flimsy hospital gown, which will be removed when I reach the operating room. I am transferred from my bed onto a stretcher, tied to it, and wheeled through the halls and down the elevator to the floor of operating rooms. I watch the ceiling, full of silver and fluorescent light, as on my back I glide by.

In the operating room I am transferred from the stretcher to the operating table. Lying on my back all I can see is my distorted reflection in the metallic light fixture, similar to that above a dentist's chair. Nurses, doctors, the anesthetist all come in and out of the room, preparing everything they will need. Everyone is wearing the same hospital green, not lime, not olive, wearing thin green gloves, has masks dangling from their necks on elastic strings.

Since everyone is dressed alike I do not know who is who, can only imagine what role each will play. It is a nurse who comes over and hooks me up to intravenous. This nurse wears a mask and on her forehead is a colored dot that identifies her as being from India. She sticks the intravenous needle into my arm.

It is the anesthetist who tells me that she will be attaching a tube to the intravenous bottle, feeding me something that will make me even more groggy than I already am. Although I have yet to see him, I know Dr. Milgram has arrived. I know because of the nurses' surprised reactions. They haven't seen him in such a long time. This patient must be someone special.

I am told that Dr. Robbins will be late, the surgery must be postponed. I am transferred, along with my intravenous bottle, to another room to await Dr. Robbins's arrival. Dr. Milgram, dressed in street clothes including his customary bow tie, comes to me in this room and tells me that he is concerned by something on the X ray taken yesterday. It seems that another tumor has grown. Or is it a shadow? He cannot tell for sure and won't know until they have opened up my thumb. He tells me Dr. Robbins has been called to an emergency and is expected to arrive within the hour.

An elderly woman is wheeled into the room and placed next to me. She is alternately screaming and mumbling words I cannot understand. She might be still for a moment, then, suddenly she makes frantic motions with her arms. I barely can make out her complaint that the cast on her leg is causing her a great amount of pain. No one pays any attention to her or to her complaint. I lie on my back next to her, as helpless as she, the intravenous attached to my arm.

After what seems to be an hour but is not even ten minutes according to the clock on the wall in front of me, the elderly woman is wheeled away, still mumbling, still screaming. A nurse comes by and tells me the woman is here to have her cast removed. She had broken her leg, and because she is very frail they thought it best to do this simple procedure in the safety of the operating room—just in case.

I watch the second hand travel around the clock. I watch it circle again and again. The temperature of the room goes from hot to cold and back to hot. I want to call the nurse, to tell her to cancel everything, I do not want to have the surgery today.

The elderly woman is wheeled back into the room. She is still mumbling, still screaming. She is no longer making those frantic motions with her arms. A few minutes or an hour later she is, once again, wheeled away. I realize that I haven't eaten or drunk anything in over sixteen hours. I watch the intravenous drip from the bottle, travel slowly, methodically, down the narrow tube into my arm. I follow drip after drip after drip.

Shortly after noon, almost three hours after I was taken into this room with the clock, I am wheeled back into the operating room. I pass Dr. Robbins, dressed in the familiar green, talking with Dr. Milgram, now also dressed in green, in the hallway. I am transferred back onto the operating table. The distorted reflection of myself once again comes into view.

As the anesthetist hooks up a tube to the intravenous, she tells me to look away. I do not want to look away. I want to know exactly what she is doing. I feel a cold liquid dripping, ever so slowly, into my arm.

She puts a black rubber mask over my face and tells me to breathe deep. She tells me to count from one hundred backward. I hear her voice. The reflection I see above me becomes more distorted, foggy but darker around the edges. I hear my voice counting. I hear other voices—or are they echoes?—I do not know to whom these voices belong.

∾

When I wake up I am choking. There is no oxygen, only ether. Nobody notices that I am having trouble breathing. I cough louder.

The nurse finally comes over. I tell her that I am nauseated. I feel a cast on my left hand and arm. Dr. Robbins promised I wouldn't need a cast. I am planning to go away next week with my social studies class to New Hampshire, to live with a rural family for a few days, a trip I have looked forward to all year. Will I still be able to go?

I tell the nurse that it is the smell of ether that is making me choke, that I need to be taken back to my room. "The man who is supposed to take you back to your room is late coming back from lunch," she says. "He should have been here a half hour ago." She brings me a semicircular indented plastic tray. "Just in case you need it," she tells me.

Soon, I feel as if I am going to need the indented tray that the nurse dropped at my side, but my left hand is in a cast and my right is still hooked up to the intravenous bottle, so I can't maneuver it in time.

Finally, the man who is going to take me back up to the ward comes back from lunch. The nurse points to my bed. I close my eyes and feel my bed begin to move. I open my eyes to see the ceiling, the silver and fluorescent light, once again whirring by.

When I am wheeled out of the elevator I see my parents sitting in two uncomfortable-looking chairs. They see it is me going by and they come directly over, my father behind my mother on one side of the hospital bed.

"We've been waiting for over four hours," they tell me. No one called to tell them the surgery was delayed, so they had arrived at the hospital by noon thinking that the surgery had already been completed. I want to tell them about the orderly who was out to lunch when I came to, but not having the energy I save that for later. I am glad to see them and I smile.

They tell me they saw Dr. Milgram and that the tumor was benign. A small piece of the bone had to be scooped out along with it. But the doctors do not yet have any idea what kind of tumor it actually was, or what caused it. The doctors are no longer concerned about what turned out to be a shadow on the X ray.

∾

A few months after being removed, the tumor reappears. Dr. Milgram has numerous consultations and sends frozen sections of it to laboratories worldwide, but not one has any idea what kind of tumor is growing in my left hand.

Dr. Robbins wants to replace the infected metacarpal with bone from my hip. To this idea Dr. Milgram replies: "Why would you redecorate a burning house?" Every time surgery seems necessary the swelling in my thumb goes down, only to grow again.

My father, upon the recommendation of his boss, takes me to Dr. Ralph Luskin at New York University Medical Center, who, according to a letter to Dr. Milgram in my medical file, diagnoses the tumor as osteomyelitis of the first left metacarpal, a diagnosis that Dr. Milgram has already discarded. Dr. Luskin recommends a further biopsy and if no pathogen can be found advises a course of intravenous antibiotics for a six-week period. His letter to Dr. Milgram ends: "This young man has a serious disability affecting both lower extremities on a congenital basis and every effort should be made to control the problem in the left thumb."

Dr. Milgram thinks it unnecessarily risky to expose me to highly toxic antibiotics. Always cautious, he puts off surgery until it is absolutely necessary. When I was young, not wanting to disturb my growth plates, he would postpone surgery on my right leg until he was sure I had grown the most I was going to grow. Later, he could not figure out a way to rotate my right foot into the normal weight-bearing position without cutting the bone, which would increase the length discrepancy between my legs. Dr. Milgram is secure enough to tell us when he does not have an answer, when there is something that he does not know.

When I turn seventeen and enter Brandeis University in Waltham, Massachusetts, ten miles west of Boston, I still have a tumor growing in my hand. In unfamiliar surroundings, assigned to the dorm with the baseball team, I do well in classes and meet new friends, but questions about how people I meet might react to my disability begin to plague me. I overhear my roommate say living with me is like living in a hospital. How do I face my roommate when I know he feels this way? There is no Helen to talk with down the hall. I walk the campus all night long.

Just as I had imagined that my missing toes would be born from my big toe, as a child I needed to create a myth that would explain, at least to my satisfaction, not only why I was born with a deformed lower body, but why I had to suffer through so much pain. There had to be a reason. And the reason had to be large enough to drown out the physical pain, as well as all the fear, confusion, and isolation I must have been feeling at the time, but never had an opportunity to express.

I began to believe that my deformed body and the pain it caused me were a sign from God that I was important. More than important, that my suffering was part of a master plan. That my suffering had meaning not only for myself but for the world.

Fact: my parents had received Dr. Milgram's name from a rabbi. Fact: I was never supposed to walk, and I miraculously learned to do so while wearing two casts. Fact: Christ was Jewish, wasn't he?

❧

"We can get purple microdots," Helen, my only personal reference point to the sixties, says. She is telling me about the infamous LSD supply made in the labs at MIT. It is parents weekend during my freshman year at Brandeis, and because my parents have a wedding, Helen has come to visit instead. We buy the drug and drop acid.

We roam the campus. It is mid-October and during autumn this is a beautiful, tranquil place. What remains on the trees are dark earth colors. Dry leaves crackle beneath our feet as we walk aimlessly. I tell Helen I feel as if someone is watching us, as if we are being followed by someone making a movie of our lives.

When we make our way up to the highest place on campus I reach down and with my left hand pick up a broken branch. Holding the dry bark in my hand, I notice that my left thumb, the one from which the tumor of unknown origin had been removed a year and a half before, is dark blue.

My thumb has never turned blue before. Knowing we are on acid, I search out a trustworthy friend and ask her what my hand looks like. "It's all blue," she tells me. I find someone else I know and he, too, confirms that my left thumb has turned blue.

Helen and I go back to my dorm and crash, sleep well into the next day. When I get up it is late morning and I realize not only is my thumb no longer blue, it no longer hurts, the swelling has gone down. I can move my thumb again as I haven't been able to do for almost two years.

When Helen wakes up we talk all day. She helps me construct the drama in which the tumor in my thumb is a sure sign from God that my disability will play a role important not only to my own fate but to that of the entire world. I am now responsible for all that will transpire. At seventeen, I have found the reason not only for having been born disabled, not only for my pain and suffering, not only for the hardships my parents have had to endure, but for all who are needy in the world. Not only have I found my answer to my question of origin, but in doing so I have found everybody's answer to the unanswerable question: "Why me?" Given such a burden, I realize I have a lot of work to do.

❧

The tumor never reappears. No traces are found in subsequent X rays.

The next months, more odd things begin to happen. During meals in the student cafeteria, my hand holds a forkful of food suspended in front of my mouth. My eyes stare into the distance as if my unintelligible thoughts might be written on the cafeteria wall. Many times I have to be brought into the present moment by my bewildered friends.

One afternoon, walking home from a friend's off-campus apartment, where I've been numerous times, I get lost. I can't remember from where I am coming, can't remember the way back to my campus dorm.

I decide to see an on-campus psychologist. But instead of having the opportunity to tell someone besides Helen the new truths I am uncovering, I am given Valium.

At random moments—studying in the library, on my way to

dinner—I find it difficult to breathe. Late one night, returning to my dorm, I begin to hyperventilate. I lie down on a couch in the TV room until someone finds me. "My head feels numb," I want to tell them, but I'm not sure whether or not my words can be heard or understood. My fingers and toes go numb. Campus security takes me to the local hospital, where I am given a shot that the doctor tells me will make me relax, then taken back to my dorm room, where, alone, I try to piece together what happened only two hours earlier.

The next day is March 15, three days before my mother's birthday, and I tell my parents what happened the night before. Concerned, not only by my brief hospital stay, but also that I have begun to see a psychologist, my parents drive up from New York to see how I am doing.

After they arrive, I take them to my favorite restaurant. During the drive into Boston, I do not mention the breathing attacks, even though that is why my parents have come to see me. During dinner, none of us says a word about it, talking about my classes and my friends.

Sitting in the backseat on the drive from Boston to Waltham, it as if I am still thirteen years old and riding home from Manhattan to Brooklyn after an appointment with Dr. Milgram. Despite my doctor's decision to again postpone the surgery he has planned for years, the three of us, stalled in traffic, remain silent.

The next day we shop at Fanneuil Hall, eat dinner in the North End, and see a movie. All day the three of us act as if what has been happening the past months has been happening to someone who is not me.

It is Sunday afternoon and my parents must leave. I walk them to the door of my dorm and say good-bye. My mother is already out the door when my father turns to me.

"Are you going to be all right?" he asks.

Looking at his face I see his eyes are filled with tears.

Burrowing my head in the bulk of his chest, I hug him. Even if I could fight through my fear what would I tell my father? I have no words or insight to explain what has been going on. I am too anesthetized to heed my body's alarm.

I want him to know how afraid I am. I want him to know how I need his love more than I ever have. But I also know if I begin to talk about my panic attacks, that might trigger one, and I want to avoid embarrassing myself by not being able to breathe in front of my father. I don't want to worry him. So I tell him what I know he wants to hear. "I think I'll be okay," I say.

"We'll call you when we get home," he tells me before he leaves. From the door of my dorm I watch him walk to the car.

Later, when I talk to my parents my mother seems distant. She gets off the phone quickly, leaving me to talk with my father. This is unusual for her.

The next time we speak I ask her if there's anything wrong. "You didn't send me a birthday card," she tells me. Yes, I had forgotten.

"For my birthday this year my son gave me a breathing attack," my mother will eventually say.

∾

One night, I have been drinking way too much with my friends. Alone, I go back to my dorm room and decide to take a bunch of pills. I leave all the lights in the room on, turn the stereo to full blast, keep the door open. I am too drunk and the pills spill all over the floor. I black out.

I am revived by my friends, who find me what must be only minutes later. Robert, my best friend, is smart enough to get everyone out of the room. When we are alone he asks: "So, you have something you want to tell me?"

❧

It is spring break of my freshman year, and the panic attacks have continued despite the Valium. Every time I attempt to have a conversation about what is going on, my mother gets up and leaves the room, complaining she has a headache.

One day I have to get out of the house, and I ask my father to drive me to see Helen, who now lives in Queens. "I need to talk to her," I tell him.

My father drops me at Helen's and before I get my coat off she asks me: "You're gay, right?"

This is the first time anyone I know has used the word gay to describe what I have been feeling. How does Helen know what I have been thinking? What do I do that makes her think I am gay? Even though much of my body's tension has been relieved by Helen uttering this word, all I can tell her is that I don't know if I'm gay but think I might be in love with Robert.

"I thought so," she tells me.

Soon, my father returns to pick me up. On the drive home, we are on the Brooklyn–Queens Expressway when he asks me if I am feeling better.

"I sometimes wonder—" my father begins to say before hesitating. I wait to see if he will continue.

After a few minutes he does. "I wonder if you'll have problems with women because of your legs and will turn to men."

"One thing has nothing to do with the other," I assure him, ending our conversation for the day. But even though what my father said makes no sense to me, the tension in my neck has returned. I sweat. My stomach begins to churn.

That summer, even though I am seeing a psychologist in New York City, I do not tell her that I have fantasies about having sex with Robert. Only during our last session before I return to Brandeis do I finally tell her I've been having sex with my childhood friend, Bill. "It was only sex," I tell her. "I don't know if it means I'm gay."

"You'll find out," she says.

❧

Although I have had sex with men, up until now the sex has never before been connected to any conscious feeling of love. The sex I have had has been with male friends with whom I grew up. Kneeling in front of Adam I know somehow this will be different.

"I dreamt there was an Emperor Antony," I recite to Adam, while kneeling before him. I look up from the book of Shakespeare I am holding so I can see him. He is looking directly at me. I look away.

"What were you thinking?" he asks.

"I was thinking that I wanted to kiss you."

"Next time, go ahead."

He bends down so our lips can meet. I rest my head on his lap and he moves his hand through my hair.

"That time when you missed the train home and had to spend the night sleeping on my floor. I wanted you then," I confess.

"You should have said something," he says before he begins, once again, to kiss me.

❧

Kevin and I are at my parents' small summer house in the Catskills in upstate New York. He wants to see the videos they have made from their old eight-millimeter home movies. I find the tapes and pop them in the VCR.

As Frank Sinatra croons, early silent scenes from my parents' wedding play on the TV screen. We laugh at the hairstyles, the fifties fashions, the way my mother sneers at my father when he accidentally sits on her dress. The camera longingly caresses the food, the salads, the chopped liver, the challah, spread out on the dais before my just-married mother and father.

I have seen all these scenes before, including the scenes of Jeffrey's early birthday party before I was born. This time, as I watch my chubby three-year-old brother, I search for clues to his behavior. In these scenes he seems not only tentative before my father, who wields the camera, but seems unsure of himself, even of his own excitement when he is given the gift of a small washing machine.

My beehive-haired mother has to turn Jeffrey's head toward the camera, and when he expresses his excitement by quickly flapping his hands in front of him, he seems embarrassed to show how happy he is.

When I finally make my appearance in the video, I begin to notice things as if I have never seen these scenes before. When Kevin remarks that I now walk around the same way as I did when I was three, I notice that my limp then was far more pronounced than I have imagined, realize that as a boy I had an enormous amount of energy. And time after time, in scene after scene, I see my mother picking me up, playing with me, holding me—experiences to this day I still cannot feel, scenes I still cannot remember.

Watching the tape play, I think of my friend Karen. Karen and her twin brother, Louie, have a good relationship with their younger brother, Ron, who is developmentally disabled. I think of Karen telling me how when she was very young her mother sat her and Louie down and explained that Ron was just like them but that he was slower to learn things. Karen's mother told her that she and their father needed to spend extra time with Ron, since he needed them because of the way he was, and that she hoped Karen and Louie, her older children, would understand.

My parents have told me they never sat down with my brother and told him the reason why they were distracted by their newly born disabled son who was in the hospital. Would things have been different if they had?

My parents are the type of people who do not talk about things unless they are forced to do so. Both Jeffrey and I, to varying degrees, have suffered from this inherited trait. Watching Jeffrey, my parents, and I grow older as the video plays I understand how responsibility does not necessarily have to lead to guilt if it is acknowledged. I understand the power of naming.

ॐ

I cannot sleep comfortably with the sheets tucked under the corners of my bed. The sense of confinement reminds me of those stiff white sheets, so meticulously cornered and tucked, of my hospital beds.

So much of life seems to happen in a bed. From a bed I am only able to see the tops of trees, sometimes only the sky. What I hear, the noise from the street or a nearby highway, are clues, but too often the elevator I hear opening, then closing, during the night causes displacement, confusion. The view from a bed is only partial, often unreliable.

In a bed what I remember most are hands. I do not know the origins of the hands. Or when the hands begin. I'm not yet sure what the hands did. But I always remember the hands.

I am being passed from hand to hand, from one person with no face to another. I feel hands, see eyes. Their eyes are looking at my legs.

Then the hands begin searching under my blanket. Every night and every morning. When they wake me up I am angry and annoyed. Sometimes I need to escape the hands, so I get up very early, take my pillows and blanket into my parents' room, and watch cartoons on their television, keeping the volume low so I do not disturb them.

I have a dream about these hands. In the dream I am being accosted, every part of me, by hands. Each hand has one large eye. The hands begin by tickling, then pressing into my skin, harder until they begin to hurt. I begin to fight back, but as soon as I swat one hand with an eye away another takes its place. There are too many hands.

Finally, I have the rhythm down and know how to beat back the onslaught of hands. I flick them off of me as if they are flies. But they get larger and larger. By now I am punching at them, harder and harder, but still they come.

❧

The room I share with my brother Jeffrey is carpeted in orange shag. There is light beige wood paneling on the side of the bed against the wall. Another wall has dark brown cork, another glossy wallpaper of silver circles contained within black and orange squares. Against this wall is a long desk, shelving, and a dresser unit, all attached, that runs almost the entire length of the wall. All the *World Book Encyclopedia*, and all the yearbooks for every year since we first bought it, are the most prominent books on the shelves. The room has been decorated according to my brother's wishes; most of the books are mine.

Thirteen, my brother has grown to be a husky boy. He already works packing groceries at the local supermarket, saving for the car he will be able to buy, cash down, when he is old enough to drive.

Always a jittery child, he has developed nervous habits such as cocking his head back and to the right, sometimes letting out what sounds like a low moan from the back of his throat. He has become increasingly obsessed with his weight, cutting dif-

ferent diets from newspapers and magazines, until finally set-
tling on the Stillman Diet, which requires drinking eight
glasses of water a day.

We sleep on a high-riser, my brother on the main part of the
bed, against the wood-paneled wall. I sleep on the bed underneath the bed one sees during the day, the bed that needs to be
pulled out and lifted up each night. We sleep facing opposite
ends of the room.

All night I hear the onrushing swish of passing cars on the
Belt Parkway fifteen stories below the bedroom window. Occasionally a siren will sound in the distance, become louder and
louder, until it grows fainter and fainter. Although I've never
gotten out of bed to check, I am sure the sirens come from
ambulances taking patients to the emergency room in Coney
Island Hospital nearby.

The only other sounds I hear are his, coming from his disembodied voice somewhere on the other end of the bed. In the
dark he calls me names—Lucretia or Fidget, freak of nature or
Lucille. When I ask him what a Fidget is he tells me it's a cross
between a fuck and a midget.

He tells me about his school, how in a few years when I go to
junior high school it will be different from elementary school
because you move from class to class, not staying in one room
the entire day. He tells me the places near the school where you
can go and eat at lunchtime. And he tells me about Tony's, the
small toy store on a corner a block away from the school.

"Mommy says Eve can come over after school tomorrow," I
tell him.

"Who's Eve?"

"My best friend. A girl."

"You don't have any friends," he tells me. "They just feel
sorry for you."

Then, he tells me I am too small. For this I have already

prepared an answer. "It's not that I'm small," I tell him, "it's that everybody else is big."

He tells me that I won't grow any more because when he jumps over me when I'm lying down that stops me from growing. In order for me to get bigger he has to jump back over me. Only then will I be able to grow.

"You better be good," he says.

I close my eyes, trying to hear my father snoring in the other room, so close to ours, but no matter how hard I try I cannot hear him. Instead I imagine the small corner store near my brother's school that is filled with all kinds of toys.

∾

When I am not yet twelve, Jeffery, fifteen, is paid twenty-five cents an hour to baby-sit for me when my parents go out at night. He leaves a sheet of paper for them in the kitchen and they sign in and sign out, marking the times to the nearest fifteen minutes, just as my brother orders.

As soon as they leave he begins.

I am watching sports on TV in my parents' bedroom when he comes in. After a growth spurt, Jeffrey already stands close to six feet tall. He no longer has a weight problem; his nervous habits have persisted. He has recently taken up annoying my mother by purposely mispronouncing words.

Jeffrey changes the channel. "You don't need to watch men running on a field," he tells me. He forces me to move over to my mother's side of the bed, farther from the TV. I do not want to watch what he is watching but I know there is no use to complain.

I leave and call Eve from the living-room phone. I am talking with Eve only a few minutes when I hear the click that tells me my brother is listening on the extension in my parents' room. I can hear the sound-tracked TV laughter filter through the phone.

Soon, I know my brother will somehow interrupt the conversation. He has done it before. He will either make cooing sounds into the phone or start to loudly contradict anything that I am saying. When he does this I am embarrassed and find some excuse and get off the phone.

I do not know how the assault begins. Perhaps I confront him about what he has just done. Perhaps I am just passing my parents' door on the way into the other room. The reason does not matter. It is not important. It is just an excuse for what happens next to happen. Angry words are said, the usual names are called.

The carpet burns my skin as my brother drags me by my neck into the living room. He pins my arms down and sits on top of me. He drools and spits in my face. Or he bends down and licks me. When I try to escape he turns me over, pulls down my pants, and takes a hard bite out of my ass.

By this time I am probably screaming. If I am strong enough that day I get away from him and bang on the metal door, just a short distance away. When I bang on the door all I hear is the banging's echo down the apartment-building hall. No one ever hears my banging, or my screaming, or if they do nobody seems to care.

When I escape back to my parents' room I go to the telephone. I cannot think whom to call so when he approaches me I take the phone and throw it at him. This rips the phone cord from the wall. The phone doesn't hit him but makes a loud ring as it hits the floor. Or, perhaps, I throw the lamp that stands at the side of the bed on my mother's night table. When I throw the lamp at my brother the arm of the female figure who holds a basket full of flowers is broken. But the lamp does not hit him, either.

"Look what you've done," my brother tells me, "you've broken it."

It is not clear what happens next. Somehow the attack escalates. Or, perhaps, it stops. I do not know because I cannot remember. All I know is later, after I am finished composing myself on the living-room couch, where I've gone to nurse my wounds, or come out of the bathroom, where I've kept myself behind the locked door, after my crying has subsided and I have caught my breath again, going back to my parents' room I notice my brother has fallen asleep on his bed.

I go back into my parents' bedroom and turn the TV on. I listen for the elevator in the hallway, the familiar steps, the key turning in the door.

∾

Over fifteen years later, I am eating lunch with my father at the Ukrainian National Home on Second Avenue in the East Village when I finally ask him how he managed after I was born. His answer: "Your mother managed."

From what I am able to glean from him, and from others who were around at the time, my father would take long walks, would often seem as if in a fog, not knowing where to turn, what might be the proper direction.

"I'm very concerned about will happen to you when we're gone," my father says, putting into words something I know he thinks about now that he is getting older.

"I think about that, too," I say. "My body doesn't look like it will be getting any better."

"I wish you and your brother—" He stops himself in midsentence.

"There's a lot you don't know," I say, hoping this does not lead into the long conversation we have never had.

"Your mother and I don't understand why you don't talk to each other."

"You don't want to understand." I realize I am angry. "Things happened between us that I'm sure you don't want to know."

My father recites the three reasons he and my mother give themselves for my brother and I not being close: "You never liked each other. He was jealous of you. You both wanted your own room."

"He abused me."

"You mean physically?" he asks. I sit on the other side of the table looking at him until he adds, "Sexually?"

"Yes."

"How?"

"I don't know yet. It's not easy for me to talk about. Not even in therapy."

"Are you sure?"

"Yes. I'm sure."

I know what I have just told him will not be easy for him to keep from my mother. Nor will telling her be a simple thing. After a long pause I ask him, "Will you tell Mom?"

"You should tell her."

"I don't want to tell her until I'm ready. I didn't want to tell you yet, but when you brought up the subject I had to tell the truth," are the only words I can offer as some kind of apology for hurting my father, for causing the confusion and pain I see so clearly in his eyes.

True to form, my father's mood outwardly changes even though I know he must be thinking about what I have told him. Instead we talk about other things. We finish lunch without saying anything else on the subject.

When we part I feel both relieved and saddened at what has transpired. But when I reach my friend's loft where I am staying, I, too, like my father, show no signs of having just crossed over a line I never imagined I would cross over today.

As I talk to my friend, I think about my father on the train ride home and want to take back the words I spoke to him in the restaurant not even an hour ago.

☙

Almost two years later, I walk into a small consulting room reserved for this occasion. My mother sees the sheaf of notes I am holding. "Looks like you're going to give one of your readings," she says. Not wanting to laugh, I look at my psychiatrist and my social worker instead. I sit across from the sofa on which my parents sit, look down at the notes shaking in my hand.

Reading from my notes I begin to spell out, as clearly as I can, the reasons we are meeting in this room at Beth Israel Hospital in Boston, the reasons I needed to check myself into 2 East, the voluntary psych ward, a week ago.

I tell my parents the facts I know about the abuse, verbal and physical, to which I was subjected by my brother. I need an encouraging look from both my psychiatrist and social worker to continue.

"And we thought you were going to tell us you had AIDS," my mother says, taking advantage of the pause.

I ask my parents why they never stopped my brother from harming me.

"We didn't know," they say in unison.

"You had to know," I say as firmly as I can. "Why do you think the lamp beside your bed—and the telephone—were broken?"

"I don't remember," my father says softly.

My mother begins to speak but before she can say even one word my father interrupts her.

"Why don't you let her talk," I demand.

The next day I am eating brunch with my parents in a

Coolidge Corner deli. When I use the word "incest" my father says, "What do you mean 'incest'? Did he penetrate you?"

I see my mother's face turn white. When I look at her she looks away. "This is too difficult for Mom," I say.

My mother looks at me and says, "Yes, this is very difficult, but if this is what we need to do for you to get better then this is what we're going to do." And I fill in the details of what I remember about how my brother treated me when I was young.

Two weeks later, back home in Provincetown, I am on the phone with my parents. I confront my father with the fact that he, too, was violent with my brother and me when we were young. When I use the word "abuse" he bristles.

"What do you mean 'abuse'?" he says. "My father would beat us kids when we deserved it."

"No one deserves it," I hear myself reply.

"I wasn't violent with them when they were young, was I, Joan?" he asks my mother, who has been listening on the other phone.

"Yes, you were," she answers.

∾

In a drawer in the night table at the side of my father's side of the bed is a vibrator. It is black with a silver head and has various red plastic attachments to use when massaging different parts of the body. There is an attachment with prongs for your scalp, a curved one for your feet. My father uses the flat one to massage his back, which he injured while serving in the navy in the 1950s.

I am just thirteen, my brother sixteen, and we are on my parents' bed watching TV. My parents are visiting Charlotte and Sam, Helen's parents, down the hall. My brother takes out my father's vibrator, places the cup-shaped attachment on the metallic head. He turns it on.

Before I know what is happening my brother has lowered my pajamas and placed the head of the vibrator on my penis. I begin to feel a strange sensation. My penis feels warm inside, as if hot liquid is moving up and down between my legs.

The machine makes too much noise. It reminds me of the noise I hear behind me at the end of a haircut when the barber shaves my neck with his razor. When the red attachment falls off, which it often does when you press too hard, the noise gets even louder. But this feels so different, too good, and I do not mind the noise.

My brother holds the vibrator's head on my penis. With one ear I try to listen to check if I can hear my parents' footsteps returning down the hall. The sensation I feel now changes. It feels as if I'm burning, then as if I'm going to pee.

Afraid I'll wet the bed I tell my brother to stop, but he does not stop. He is laughing as he presses the head of the vibrator, the cup-shaped red attachment, harder on my penis. When he does this the vibrator makes an even louder noise, metal grating against metal, as if the machine is angry.

The noise, the burning, the fear my parents will soon come home—and I try to squirm away from the machine my brother holds. I use my hand to fend him off. When I try to pull my pajama bottom back on is when I first see it. I do not know where my brother is—perhaps he's putting the machine back in my father's drawer, or perhaps he, too, is afraid at what he sees. On my penis, on the delicate, thin-skinned ridge where the head meets the shaft, is blood.

❧

In my parents' apartment on Cropsey Avenue in Brooklyn, next to the piano, on an easel in a corner near the doorway to the kitchen stands an enlarged painting-size photograph. The photograph was taken at my brother's bar mitzvah in May 1970, when I was nine and a half years old. The photograph is heavily framed with dark brown wood.

In this photograph, which I have often asked my parents to remove, I am pictured with my brother. We are both dressed in light blue striped suits, both with white shirts and light blue bow ties. It is shot quite close and we both gaze out past the viewer. My posture seems stiff, my smile forced. If you follow our gaze you would look directly over your right shoulder to see what it is we are looking at.

We are posed close to each other—my head seemingly grazes Jeffrey's upper chest, gently. The photograph shows me to be a head and a half shorter than my older brother. Since my body above the waist is of normal length, and broad, this photograph, cropped just above my ribs, provides the illusion of my standing as tall as your average nine-and-a-half-year-old boy. This illusion is made possible by the fact that when photographed I was standing on a chair.

When visiting my parents, what does my brother think of this photo? Of its prominent display? If we were ever able to talk about it what is it that we would say?

There is another photograph. Since rescuing this photograph from my parents' haphazardly organized photo drawer, I have kept it inside my wallet for years. This photograph was taken when I was in the third grade, not too long before the photograph in my parents' living room was taken. In this head shot I am eight years old, wearing a white shirt with light blue lines that break into a floral design, patterned in columns, on the body of the shirt, as well as on the collar.

The background is that familiar nondescript hazy color field in all my school photos. The color is close to the sky blue we see if we are awake at dawn. The blue sets off my olive skin, as does the whiteness of my shirt and my toothy, even then slightly ironic, smile, emphasizes the otherworldliness of the photo while at the same time grounding my earnest happiness, which seems suspended in time. The look in my eyes matches my smile. My straight dark brown hair, the bangs, the sides, as well as in the back, is slightly too long.

Even when not looking at it, this photograph I easily remember. I have kept it with me, in fact and in spirit, to remind myself of the inherent optimism and innocence that is reflected in those sweet yet headstrong eyes and smile.

Years after more surgery, emotional awareness, and just plain old growing up, this photograph now safely resides in a scrapbook kept in a drawer in my study. I always know where it is. I still use it as a reference point, a reflection of a state of mind—of being—I can never replicate, but, perhaps, can still emulate by remembering.

This photograph, and my interpretation of it, is, too, perhaps, in its own way an illusion. Can the truth be located somewhere between this photograph in my scrapbook and the photograph my parents refuse to remove from their living room? If I look at them side by side, for a long enough time, what changes in each would I discern? Would what I was feeling underneath that frozen stare, that happy smile, be revealed? Which photograph is the greater lie?

∾

During my freshman year at Brandeis I go to see my friend Barry, a chemistry major who works in the lab. Barry and I have become friends by going to the dog track in Revere, following the New York Mets together, drinking in the campus pub. The first time I go to see Barry in the lab I begin to feel dizzy, lightheaded, in the hall. Then my body heats up, my head pulses, I sweat. I quickly walk outside and sit down on the Chemistry Building stairs.

The college chemistry labs smell like the hospital. The slightly metallic, slightly sour smell of ether pervades the halls.

The next semester I have a class that is held in the same building as the labs. Since that time I went to see Barry I have not been inside that building, always calling Barry on the phone when I want to visit, asking him to meet me outside. I spend the hour before the first class trying to map out a route that will bypass the hallway where I had trouble months before.

Unable to find an odorless route I finally hold my breath and walk the shortest distance possible, and by the time I reach my class I am sweating, my heart is pounding, racing—I allow myself to breathe for the first time only when the lecture-hall door is closed firmly behind me. I learn to keep a Valium handy, outside of the vial, in my shirt pocket. If I need help breathing, I can place it under my tongue to be absorbed into my system faster than if I swallow.

∾

When my right knee begins to bother me during my senior year, I put off going to see Dr. Milgram, now over eighty, who sees fewer and fewer patients in the small office to which he has been relegated in the newly built Hospital for Joint Diseases downtown on Second Avenue. Even the thought of picking up the phone to call his secretary has me flushed with fear. Finally, I make an appointment to see my doctor, whom I have not seen for many years.

Just thinking about walking into the hospital is enough to start a panic attack. Not wanting to go alone, and not knowing who else to ask, I ask my father to come with me. We meet outside.

Even outside the hospital, where many doctors and nurses buy food at the hot dog stand, the by now well-known symptoms begin. The sight of white coats, that familiar surgery green, has me smelling ether even before I walk through the revolving door. The announcement system calls a doctor to emergency. While waiting for the elevator I begin to have trouble breathing. My palms are sweating. Inside the elevator they are so wet I need to ask my father to open my bottle of pills. I have never reacted this way inside a hospital. My father has never seen me this way before.

"Are you going to be okay?" my father asks as we stand waiting for me to catch my breath outside the elevator on Dr. Milgram's floor. "Take it easy," he offers. I nod my head, waiting for the pill to take effect.

When I see Dr. Milgram, he looks old, tired. Sitting behind his desk, he looks from my file, then at me, trying to jog his memory, but he can't seem to remember who I am.

No longer having an examination room, Dr. Milgram looks at my legs in his office. Naked from the waist down I stand in front of him as he examines my knees. Seeing my legs, he seems to remember.

"Walk for me," he gruffly demands, and I do so, lifting up my shirttail so he can see what he needs to see.

"Where have you been?" he asks. I tell him what I've done in school. "You're doing fine," he asserts, whether to me or to himself I do not know. It is then I begin to cry.

"You don't know how hard it's been," is what I want to say, what I want to tell him still. I want to spill my guts, tell him everything I've held inside for twenty years, but all I can do is sob.

I do not remember anything else about that visit. I know my knee still bothered me, at times giving me a sharp pain, then feeling as if it weren't there to support my weight. I do know it was soon after I last saw Dr. Milgram that I decided I needed to learn to drive a car so it would be easier for me to get around.

The next-to-last entry in my medical records, dated April 21, 1981, written in Dr. Milgram's almost illegible hand, reads: "Right knee discomfort. Knee is stable. The knee 90 degree ext. not due to femoral presc. in hip. An osteotomy would be needed to align the knee. Could foot be affected? If vasculatory permits. Martin Fischer will study and report."

I did go see Dr. Fischer, who, by having me drink some kind of dye, mapped out the vasculatory pathways in my leg, just as he mapped out the tumor in my left thumb years before.

In the records there is a Xerox of a Polaroid photograph, copied on Dr. Martin Fischer's stationery, dated April 21, 1981. In the photo I am standing in front of an open door. I am lifting my pants legs, exposing both my knees. I am wearing a dark sweater with three bands of white stripes, two of an inter-locking diamond design, across my chest and shoulders. I look straight at the camera, my curly hair too long. There is the slightest trace of a smile. A calendar picturing an X ray of someone's hand, palm up, is on the wall.

In the records there is one final entry, dated June 26, 1984. "Called patient," it reads. "No answer."

T W O

Heat and White Stone

I needed to find out who I was told I was
before I could contradict it.

—JO SPENCE

$\mathcal{F}$OR most of my life I have lived near water. When I wake in the middle of the night and cannot get myself back to sleep the sound of foghorns, sometimes distant, sometimes near, serves as the background for my fast-moving thoughts. No matter from what distance the foghorns sound, they are persistent and in their constancy echo throughout my body louder and louder the longer I remain awake.

During these sleepless nights the drone of the foghorns is transformed into sounds unlike those that originally enter through the walls, through the windows, into my room. On the hottest nights, when I wake on top of the sheets, the warning sounds of the foghorn become the arresting notes of the shofar, the ram's horn blown by the cantor, awakening us to a new year on Rosh Hashanah, the sounds that end the holy fast of Yom Kippur.

Tikiyah . . .

Teruah . . .

Tikiyah . . .

And if I listen long and carefully enough, I can once again hear the Arabic prayers broadcast from the mosque on the Temple Mount in Jerusalem during the holy month of Ramadan, the melodic chanting so similar to the plaintive wails of prayer I heard in synagogues when I was young. These mysterious yet familiar tones ride from the minarets on the hot night air into my room, just as they did every night during my stay in Israel over a decade ago.

❧

El Al tells you to get to JFK Airport two and one half hours early. It is 1984 and although there has not been a recent terrorist attack on an airplane, El Al takes every precaution.

As passengers enter the terminal they are accosted by the Lubavitcher Jews, religious Hasidim. I am reminded of the Mitzvah Mobile that roamed my neighborhood when I was young, carrying Hasidim who sought out assimilated Jewish boys whom the religious sect would try to convince to lay tefillin, the black boxes with Torah parchment inside, wear yarmulkes, would proselytize us to study the Torah, to be more observant Jews. These men with *tzitzis*, the fringes of the *tallis*, the Jewish prayer shawl, hanging out from beneath their white shirts, were comforts to our parents, who lived in fear that their secular teenage children would be converted by the Jews for Jesus who would make regular appearances in our apartment-building hallways and at our door.

I would avoid the men in the Mitzvah Mobile, running back indoors when I saw their white van parking on Cropsey Avenue or Bay Forty-third Street. These zealous men, wearing unkempt beards and *payis*, unshaven curls dangling near their ears, terrified me in ways I was much too young to understand.

As passengers congregate in the security area I realize that I have not been among a group where everyone is Jewish since the last time I was in synagogue, eight years ago. When with a group of disabled people I feel we should disperse before passersby throw money at us. Together with all these Jews, I cannot help thinking we will be rounded up, put on planes instead of trains.

"Has anyone given you any package to take to Israel? Has anyone else packed your luggage? Have you accompanied your luggage the entire time since leaving your home? What languages do you speak?"

This last question stops me. "I speak some Hebrew," I tell the security team.

"Why do you speak Hebrew?"

"I studied it in school," I tell them, shrugging my shoulders for the benefit of my parents, who have driven me to the airport and are standing at the other end of the baggage check, waiting for me to be cleared.

"Who do you know in Israel?"

"The person I will be staying with and a few old family friends."

"Why are you going to Israel?"

The truth is I never wanted to go to Israel until six months ago. When I was young my father would badger me with the myths of Israel: the importance of having a place, a homeland, where Jews could always go; the Arab hatred that besieged the young country; how the Jews miraculously transformed the desert into paradise.

"They'll always hate you for being Jewish," my father told me when I was young.

"Then I won't be Jewish," was my naive, petulant reply.

"If the Nazis were here you'd be Jewish. No matter what you say, no matter what you do, you'll always be Jewish."

For this I had no verbal response. But as a teenager I watched in silent terror when the young developmentally disabled daughter in the TV miniseries *Holocaust* was sent to her death because of her disability. I knew the Nazis would have killed me first for being disabled. Soon, I learned about the pink triangle and added being gay to this list of expendable undesirables.

Since my bar mitzvah, the culmination of my years in

Hebrew school, I had little interest in Judaism. The religion did not answer my questions related to my disability.

When I was in the hospital my father would ask the rabbi to come and visit me. When I was young this felt comforting. But by the time I was in the hospital having the tumor in my thumb removed it no longer made any sense. My father told me he went to the synagogue, to make a *misheberech*, a prayer for health, for wellness. I challenged my father's good intentions by asking him, "Why did God make me this way in the first place?" Years later, even all the genetic advances of science do not silence this question lurking in our minds.

No one took my questions seriously enough to engage me in a dialogue about religion that could draw me closer to my inherited faith. Growing up, I needed easy answers. But Judaism, unlike other religions, is a religion of argument and questions, not answers. The Talmud, the interpretation of the laws of the Torah, is just as important as the laws themselves. I felt unmoored when my Hebrew school teacher told us that the Bible stories we studied were parables, might not have happened at all.

The reason I went to Brandeis, named for the Jewish Supreme Court justice and the first American university founded by Jewish money, was because I did not get into Cornell. And also, the history of radicalism on the Brandeis campus during the 1960s made it sound like a good place to go.

But when I moved to California after graduate school I began to crave an understanding of my Jewish identity. Perhaps it was the fact that in San Francisco I had to use personal days to observe Rosh Hashanah and Yom Kippur, unlike the automatic days off from work in New York. Perhaps it was that I now knew enough to be able to separate the religion from the culture. Or perhaps it was the distance in miles and time I now had from my past, enabling me to make my Jewishness my own.

This distance also caused a rootlessness, a common feeling

when you live in California. And every now and then I experienced a subtle anti-Semitism—"He's Jewish and he's proud," a co-worker told her friend in my presence when I was planning my trip to Israel. I had to explain what a Passover seder was to my bosses.

But I do not have the time to explain all this to the uninterested security team even if I were able. "I've always wanted to go," I offer to the man and woman in uniform, not knowing what else to say.

My answers cause the security team enough concern. I watch other passengers in back of me on line pass through as the security team riffles through my now opened backpack.

"At least they didn't let me off easy because I'm disabled," I tell my parents when I rejoin them after my okayed luggage is sent on its way to the plane.

I hug my mother good-bye, and thank her for the Magen David, the Jewish star she wore when she was a young girl, which she gave me when I asked if she had a Jewish star that I could wear around my neck, along with the amethyst I bought as a travel present to myself at Bones of Our Ancestors, a hippie gem shop on Haight Street in San Francisco.

"Be careful," my mother says, her usual parting admonition.

Then it is my father's turn and when he bends down to kiss me I notice he is crying.

"I'll be fine," I assure him both verbally and with a hug. "You have Micha's number," I remind him.

As I walk through one last metal detector and down the long ramp to the plane I feel my father's eyes watching me. The farther I go the heavier is his presence, an increasing pressure just below the hairline on my neck.

Turning around for one last wave good-bye, I see my mother with her arm around my father, his eyes as bright as if they were right in front of me. I think of how during my year in London he checked the exchange rates and the London weather daily and I realize that his tears are not tears of worry, nor tears of concern. Turning back around to head toward the gate I know that the trip I am about to take is a journey that my father has always wanted to take, a trip my mother would like to take as well. But this remains a trip they have not yet taken. Instead, it is I, their youngest son, who is making the trip to Israel.

As I continue to walk down the ramp it is as if my father's spirit has entered my body. As I approach the gate I see the awaiting plane. I travel to Israel wearing my mother's Jewish star, as my father's son.

❧

When I made my travel plans I decided I wanted to fly to Israel not on TWA or United, but on the overnight flight on El Al. During the flight I talk to the flight crew in the rudimentary Hebrew I learned in Hebrew school, the language that has remained unused, dormant, since I barely passed the required foreign-literature course during my sophomore year in college.

On the plane I fall asleep until the stewardess, serving bagels and lox, wakes me. Down the narrow aisle at the front of the plane, I see three bearded men, two stocky and overweight, one lanky and tall, each dressed in the familiar Orthodox garb, black suit, white shirt, and black hat, each holding an open book I know to be the Siddur, each wearing a set of tefillin secured to the head and left arm by black leather straps ritually wrapped around both arm and head, the tefillin I refused to place on my body, ignoring my paternal grandmother's bribes, the money she would give me if I would perform this sacred rite.

As I eat my bagel I watch the three bearded men bend their head slightly, like my father standing next to me in synagogue did on Shabbas mornings, on Rosh Hashanah and Yom Kippur, sometimes unexpectedly bending at the knee, all in rhythm with their mumbled Hebrew words. I notice that they are facing the left side of the plane, davening toward the twice destroyed temple in Jerusalem.

Two hours later we have landed. What will people think of me—a disabled, gay, secular American in Israel? On the streets of Jerusalem will I be met with the same stares which greet me back home?

The strains of "Yerushalayim Shel Zahav" (Jerusalem, City of Gold) play over the audio system as the plane taxis to the gate at Ben Gurion Airport, just outside of Tel Aviv, where my friend Micha will be waiting.

I met Micha, the youngest son born just after World War II to Dutch Holocaust survivors, a year ago, when he was on an internship in San Francisco. We became friends and I helped him type up his final report on counseling alcoholics. Before returning home he invited me to come stay with him in Israel. Master's degree in theater from Columbia in hand, with my first chapbook of poems published that spring, and my first play scheduled to begin rehearsals at LaMama, the experimental theater in New York, next fall, I decided to use the money my paternal grandmother put aside for when I got married, and take Micha up on his offer.

My pack on my back, I am halfway through the crowded line and there is still no sign of Micha. I look up at the cloudless sky, at the unwavering palm trees standing perfectly still in the noontime heat. This could be Florida. Or New Mexico. Any place with little shade and an unrelenting sun. Traveling by plane does this to you. Upon arrival at your destination your body has little sense of having traveled so far, your mind does not translate the signals of where, actually, you are.

Finally, at the very end of the three-deep row of faces, is Micha. "Shalom chaveri," he says as we hug hello. "I'm so glad you are here."

He takes my pack from me and carries it toward a line of

taxis. Micha speaks too quickly for me to understand his exchange with the driver.

"I have a meeting in Tel Aviv. David, he's a tall Canadian, will meet you where I tell the driver to leave you. Here are the keys. I'll see you for dinner."

On the highway to Jerusalem we pass dry, barren land filled with large rocks and boulders. As the road begins the ascent to the city I notice the walls that line the road are built with these same large rocks. Close up I realize these rocks are white stone.

When we enter the city the buildings are built with the same white stone. The driver maneuvers from a main street to a narrow side street that ends in a parking lot filled with cars. At the other end of the lot I see a tall balding man reading a book as he leans against a short stone wall.

The driver stops near the man and retrieves my backpack from the rack on top of the taxi. I dig into my front pocket for some of the Israeli money my father gave me before I left New York.

"I'll get that," says a voice behind me. I recognize the accent as sounding slightly British.

When I turn around I see the voice belongs to the tall man I noticed reading.

"I'm David," the man tells me as he lifts my pack. "I live close to Micha's. I'll show you where he lives and tell you how to find me. When you're ready why don't you come by and I'll fix you something to eat," he says. "You must be hungry."

As we leave the parking lot the street, surrounded by walls, begins to narrow. We are walking on large flat stones. "Welcome to the Old City. This is the Jewish Quarter," David tells me.

❧

Micha's house has three stories built around a central enclosed skylit courtyard. The entrance floor is the oldest, dating back to Crusader times. Beyond a stone arch there is a room he uses for the laundry and another room that is used by his roommate, Shabtai, a Bulgarian Jew originally from Sofia.

To the right is the stairway which leads to the second-story landing. From there you can go left across the landing to Micha's room or turn right into the living room. Off the living room to the left is the kitchen, from which leads another stairway up to the open rooftop patio. Up on the roof it is as if you are in Los Angeles, except for the view only a few streets away: the Al Aksa Mosque and the golden Dome of the Rock on the Haram al-Sharif, the Temple Mount, and below it the Western Wall. On a day as clear as the day I arrive you can see all the way to Jordan.

I have settled in and follow the verbal directions to David's, across the Jewish Quarter. As I walk I try to notice landmarks—the Burnt House, the ice-cream café, the most recent excavations—in order to facilitate my return. In front of the excavation site shouting children play. As I pass them I am relieved they are too immersed in their game to notice me. After a long day of travel I want to put off what I'm sure will be questioning stares.

During lunch, David, originally from Canada, tells me of his on-again, off-again relationship with Micha.

"It's not easy being gay here," he tells me.

"Why is that?" I ask.

"With all the issues of security, there is a strong emphasis on having a family—in addition to all the Jewish stuff that implies. Even Micha, who is more out than any of us—he goes on the radio, could you believe it?—grapples with these issues. I don't know if you can be both happy and gay."

I wonder if David means this as a general statement or only for gays in Israel, but I am too exhausted for this kind of conversation and I know I'll have plenty of time later for clarification.

"Micha has been so excited about having you here. You have an energy he admires."

"He's a very special man," I tell David. "But you probably know that already."

"Special and difficult," he replies.

Sounds like the way I've often been described, I think. "I admire his commitment to being a Jew," I say instead.

"And he admires your commitment to being gay."

"It isn't much of a choice."

"Neither is being a Jew."

After lunch, on my way back to Micha's I am hopelessly lost, walking down dead-end streets where the stones are uneven, rougher. Streets that seem like alleys. No street leads me where I want to go.

I sit down against a wall, attempting to summon my usually good sense of direction. What seems like a perfect piece of cooked meat is comfortably lodged in between two stones near the intersection of an alley and a larger though still-empty street.

I stop again and try to listen for the echoes of the young children who were playing near the excavation site, knowing that from there I would be able to find the café, the Burnt House, the turn around a bend to Micha's door. I strain to hear the children's call, follow them back to the open plaza, where I see the excavation site, which is close to where I began, in front of David's door.

Now, I am successful. Back at Micha's I take a nap and wait for his return.

"You found everything okay?" he asks when he comes home.

"Fine," I tell him. "When I was walking back from David's I saw this piece of cooked meat lying in the middle of the street."

"They leave poisoned scraps of food to kill the cats who stray from the Arab Quarter into the Jewish Quarter," he tells me nonchalantly as he begins to prepare dinner. "David and I have been lovers, but recently it's changed between us and he thinks he wants to go back to Canada. He might return home by the time you leave.

"It isn't easy being gay here," he continues, repeating what David told me this afternoon. There's such an emphasis on having children, a family, to continue the people. And with all the tension a family is something that at least feels secure."

I wonder if this is the party line or just something that Micha and David have come to. But it is too early in my stay to just blurt out such a question to my host. I am determined I will find the answer to this question on my own.

ᘛ

"Do you want to go visit the Wall?" Micha asks me after we have finished the late dinner he has served.

I have arrived on Yom Yerushalayim, the day celebrating the reunification of Jerusalem after the 1967 Six Day War. As we walk, Micha tells me that tonight there is supposed to be a celebration.

I notice the dark boys walking together in the plaza in front of the Wall. They arrive from a narrow street that leads from the Arab Quarter. "Through there is the souk," Micha tells me, pointing beyond the small archway that leads into the Arab market. Leisurely, these boys, perhaps fifteen or sixteen years old, maybe younger, walk in couples or groups of four or five. They hang on each other's bodies as they stroll, familiarly talking to each other in Arabic, or calling to another couple or group nearby. When one group meets another they are playful and at ease. Near the entrance to the sanctuary blocked off in front of the Wall one boy chases another, who uses the remainder of his group as an obstacle to being caught. A truce is made by the offering of a cigarette.

When we enter the partitioned area that serves as an open-air synagogue, which itself is divided according to Orthodox tradition into two sections, one for men, one for women, I am immediately transfixed by the Wall. I move closer to the white stone, close enough to see small pieces of paper rolled up and placed in the cracks between the rows. I watch a nearby Orthodox man dressed in the customary black suit, white shirt, and black hat as he prays before the Wall, and next to him a more secular-looking man whose camera protrudes over his prayer book, blocking his view. Does he read from memory?

It is difficult to imagine this wall of stones is what remains of the Holy Temple, the holiest site of Judaism, destroyed by Titus's Roman army in A.D. 70, after it was rebuilt on the same site as Solomon's Temple, which was itself destroyed by the Nebuchadnezzar-led Babylonians in 587 B.C. Both times the temple was destroyed on Tishah-b'Av, the ninth day of the Hebrew month of Av, a "coincidence" that, to me, has always stretched the meaning of the word.

I try to match what I see before me to the photos I have seen of the narrow passageway in front of the Wall, the way it appeared from 1948 until 1967, before the Six Day War, when Jews were not allowed to visit their holy site nor live in the Jewish Quarter, when Jordan ruled the Old City of Jerusalem. I stare up at the height of the wall, knowing that above it is the Temple Mount, where once the Holy Temple stood, and where today stand the Al Aksa Mosque and the Dome of the Rock, the third holiest Islamic site, first built in A.D. 691, which contains the rock believed to be where Abraham intended to sacrifice his son Isaac, and from where Muhammad ascended to heaven.

I meet Micha back in the wide plaza and he tells me he must get up early for work tomorrow so he must be getting home. "You stay," he tells me as he kisses me lightly on my forehead. I say good night and perch myself on a bench in the plaza with a clear view of the Wall.

I am watching passersby when I hear the sound of singing. As I listen more carefully I discern that the distant song has a bass accompaniment provided by the revving of motorcycles. The song comes closer and when it is loud enough to know it is just out of sight, I turn to catch the beginning of what appears to be a motorcade, motorcycles leading a crowd of joyous singing young men. Not until the motorcade has stopped in the plaza do I notice that in the center of the throng is a large black limousine, that the men are teenage boys who dance, kicking their legs, doing the *horah*, around the limousine as if the car were a bar mitzvah boy traditionally raised on his chair. I think without the limousine and motorcycles it could be the marriage scene from *Fiddler on the Roof*, but remind myself this is the Middle East, after all.

The circle opens up into a line and the last boy at the end of the line assists someone from the backseat of the car. An old bearded man dressed in the traditional black outfit is led by the long line of boys, now dancing backward, who escort the old man to the now vacant sanctuary in front of the white-stoned Wall.

The line of dancing boys transforms itself into a wall of prayer, the old man in the center and a few steps in front of his followers. Everyone, from the archway entrance of the Arab Quarter to the street from where the throng has come, from behind me where Micha is home asleep to the Wall itself in front of me, is quiet. When I listen hard enough I can hear the ancient, rhythmic prayers as the old man dressed in black and his accompanying crowd of boys daven before the Wall.

And then they are finished and just as they came but in reverse, they *horah* the old man back to the waiting limousine, the motorcycles start their engines, and the song once again begins as they all drive off, dancing into the newer part of Jerusalem beyond the walls.

On this balmy night all is once again quiet in the plaza

before the Wall. I check my watch. It is almost two a.m. There is not another person, native or tourist, in sight. Have I been dreaming what just transpired? Was it a vision implanted by Micha's kiss into my mind?

I walk past the partition and once again approach the Wall. But this time I cannot go closer. I back up and reach behind me for a metal folding chair left out by someone who worshiped here earlier in the night. Sitting down, I know this is the same kind of chair used in our old synagogue, located above a dry cleaner on Cropsey Avenue in Brooklyn, before the newer one was built less than a block away on Bay Forty-third Street. And I realize, like countless Jewish men and women for countless years before me, I, too, am crying before the Wall.

I remember being admonished in Hebrew school not to call these stones "the Wailing Wall." I remember reading it was called the Wailing Wall not for those of us who cry in its presence, but for the dew that forms on the stones each morning. I think of Micha sleeping in his bed not far behind me. And I think of my parents, continents away, after a long day of work sitting down to a familiar table to eat dinner with each other.

The next day I learn that the dancing, singing boys were from a yeshiva and that the old squat bearded man in Orthodox garb they surrounded is the chief rabbi of Israel. The pieces of paper placed between the stones of the Wall are messages, requests of God, left by visitors to be collected early each morning before the morning minyan assembles for prayer. I do not know who receives these messages. Or if someone actually reads them. Or if they are simply thrown away.

The next morning I remain transfixed by how an ancient wall of stone, given meaning long ago by both creation and destruction, possesses the power, in its presence, to arouse so many Jews from around the world to heights of both sorrow and joy, as if we, each of us in our own life, personify the cycle of destruction and renewal, of disappointment and hope, that is the history of the people who first carried these stones and built a wall.

❧

I call Drew, a friend of a friend, and Shaoul, his lover, answers. "Come on over," Shaoul says after I tell him who gave me Drew's number. "Drew should be back soon," he says.

Micha gives me directions. "You'll enjoy Shaoul and Drew," he adds.

"You know them?"

"We all know each other here. It's one little village."

Drew and Shaoul live in a comfortable section of Jerusalem not far from the Old City. The small apartment houses are modern, most built in the late sixties or early seventies, in the explosion of building that took place not too long after the Six Day War. How do Drew and Shaoul afford to live here?

This question is partially answered when I reach their building. Their building seems older, not as finely appointed as the others. They live on the uppermost floor, the fifth, not an easy climb even when I'm not having any physical problems.

I knock on the door and Shaoul, wearing a T-shirt and a towel wrapped around his waist, opens the door. "Come in, come in," he says in an accent that I have already been able to identify as Israeli. "I'm just getting ready to go to work. Drew shouldn't be away much longer."

I enter what seems to be a one-room apartment. Clothes, which I assume have been discarded after being worn, are strewn in one corner, books are piled in another. I sit down on what must serve as both living-room sofa and bed.

"The place is a mess," Shaoul says. "Drew has been away in America and I'm not very good with the house," he tells me as he peels off his T-shirt, revealing a well-toned body whose golden brown tan matches that of his face. When he drops his towel, I have just enough time to notice his wet dark black hair that fans out on his chest and stomach before narrowing into a sparse trail that leads past his abdomen to a perfectly shaped, rather large penis, which nests in an ample supply of just as dark pubic hair. Even though I have had sex with a handful of men, I have never seen such a beautiful body so close before.

"So you're staying with Micha?" he asks as he pulls on a pair of tight-fitting underwear. "You're in the right place," Shaoul tells me. "He is very popular. He knows everyone."

"Is it because of his being on the radio?" I ask.

"Could you believe he did that? Mr. Israel Homosexual."

"I live in San Francisco," I say, as if that would explain my lack of surprise that Micha would come out on the radio.

"Drew wants us to move to San Francisco. He says I can make more money there."

"What do you do?"

"Drew's the smart one. Since being in the military, I work in a hotel as a waiter," he says as he stands before a mirror admiring himself in his work uniform of black pants and white shirt, the top buttons unbuttoned in the no-tie casual Israeli style.

"How long have you been together?" I ask.

"What do you mean?"

"You and Drew? How long have you—"

"Oh, you mean lived here."

"Yeah," I say, backtracking a bit to cover up what seems to have been taken as an inappropriate question.

"About six months. That must be Drew coming up the stairs."

When Drew enters there is no demonstration of affection between them. Have I misunderstood? Are Drew and Shaoul lovers?

"This is Kenny. Katie's friend. You're just in time. I'm going to be late for work." That said, Shaoul is out the door.

"What do you think of him?" Drew asks as he serves us tea.

"He's quite attractive." I impart the most obvious characteristic that comes to mind.

"I want him to move with me to San Francisco, but I think that scares him."

"Scares him? Why would that scare him?" I say, thinking how self-assured Shaoul seemed to be.

"Leaving his family. And the whole gay scene. No one who hasn't been there quite gets what it's like back in the States. Most of the gay men here are married to women. Only when an American is involved do they couple off."

"How long have you and he—" I hesitate, not wanting to overstep the same boundary I seemed to have crossed when I asked the same question to Shaoul.

"I met him when I was studying here three years ago. I missed him when I went home to finish up my senior year and came back as soon as I saved enough. That was six months ago."

"Are you a couple?" I venture to ask, considering that Drew has not been taken aback by my initial question.

"I think so," Drew tells me. "But things are different here. Even though gay sex is legal it is very difficult—both the culture and the money. All the inflation."

"What do you do?"

"I'm still in ulpan, studying Hebrew. A lot of Shaoul's money goes to help out his family."

"Do his parents know?"

"Are you kidding? He's their eldest son."

"Have you met them?"

"Only once. They think we're good friends. Cheap rent."

"Do you really think they don't know?"

Drew pauses and takes a long sip of tea before he answers. "I doubt it, but I honestly don't know."

On the way back to Micha's I pass through the unpopulated part of town that used to be the no-man's-land between Jordan and Israel, where the holes caused by the bullets shot between the hostile forces can still be seen in the facades of many warehouse-type buildings. I can't seem to get the thought of Shaoul, the confidence with which he displayed himself before me, as well as what he displayed, out of my mind.

Reentering the Old City I think about the pressures of Israeli society that burden these two gay men. Even though they are both my age their experience of being gay seems different from mine. How do social situations influence patterns of erotic and romantic attachment?

My brief time with Adam, who after two weekend trysts a year apart, one in London, one back in the States, has become involved with a woman, has familiarized me with bisexuality, which I still do not completely understand. But being gay and married to a woman is a step beyond. A step that necessitates negating too important a part of one's emotional life for the sake of security or propriety. A step that relegates the intimate relationship between two men to having sex.

Since Adam, though I have had sex with perhaps a dozen men, I have yet to find a man with whom I would want to build a more permanent relationship. Both Micha and David, and Shaoul and Drew, the two couples I have thus far met in Israel, have forged relationships that are shaded by an ambiguity with which I am not accustomed.

∾

I spend the next afternoon at Yad Vashem, the museum that remembers the Holocaust, located in a new section of Jerusalem, far from the city's center. The path to the museum is surrounded by hills filled with newly planted trees.

On the path I encounter a young Japanese man. We exchange names; his is Koto.

"Where are you from?" I ask.

"Outside Tokyo."

When Koto tells me he will be in Israel for an entire year I ask him what he will be doing during his stay.

"Studying Hebrew at an ulpan," he tells me.

"Are you Jewish?" I ask.

"No. No. I am interested in the Jews."

When we reach the museum Koto and I go our separate ways. Occasionally, when our paths cross again inside, we smile.

In the museum, a group of schoolboys, each with a blue woven yarmulke on his head, notices me. One elbows another, wanting his schoolmate to look at me. I respond in one of the ways I sometimes respond; I wave to them, then immerse myself in the photos displayed on the wall. I imagine the schoolboys are still watching me with expressions not unlike those of the German children who, in the photo, watch Nazi-uniformed men publicly humiliate an elderly rabbi.

The next time I look the boys are gone, but outside, after I have finished my tour of the museum, that photo of the elderly rabbi wearing a crudely made sign—JUDE—being pulled by a Nazi officer into the street by his beard, as a crowd of Aryan-looking Germans stand and watch, remains in my mind.

Dazed by the photo, almost blinded by the still-brilliant sunlight, I bump into a large object on the path. Finding my balance, I see the object is a large, narrow wooden boat. Near it is a plaque that tells me this is one of the boats the Danes used to sail Jews to safety after the Nazis invaded Denmark.

Surrounding the boat are other plaques, these on trees. Checking the map of the grounds I took from the museum, I pinpoint my location. I have entered "the Garden of Survivors," whose prominent feature is these trees, each one planted by someone who was rescued during the Holocaust in honor of the non-Jew who helped him or her escape or hide until the war was over.

Leaving the garden I think about how no mention of the Nazi persecution of other groups, not only those who were gay or disabled, but the Gypsies, the Poles, the Slavs, has a place in Yad Vashem. That this museum is a place set up to selectively remember the Jews, an attitude similar to that of my father's, is not satisfying, but considering my experience of the museum has overloaded me with emotion-packed images, I agree to accept the museum for what it offers, if just for today.

I make my way from the garden into a pavilion covered by immense planes of concrete that form triangles, a protective tent, pointing skyward. Inside, even when my eyes finally adjust to the dimmer light, it is dark. Beyond a railing are many eternal flames, each one bearing the name of a concentration camp before it. Auschwitz, Theresienstat, Bergen-Belsen . . . I hear a noise, some object hitting an obstacle, a fluttering of wings. An unseen bird is frustrated. The flapping of its wings against the concrete as it repeatedly attempts to take flight, echoes throughout the hall.

Trying to ignore the persistent noise of the trapped bird, I locate more names: Dachau, Treblinka, Sobibor . . . until I am driven from the hall by the disturbing echo of the trapped bird's wings. Outside, in the light, I try to quell my increasing sense of anxiety by revisiting the Danish boat, by trying to locate the tree planted by Micha's family in honor of the Dutch couple that hid his mother, father, older brother, and two friends. I search for the name of this ordinary family who changed another family's history, risking their own lives by hiding some Jews.

Alone at the bus stop, I keep looking up the hill to see if anyone else is coming. I check my watch, which tells me the museum will soon be closed. A bus comes but I do not get on. I look back up the hill hoping that Koto will soon appear.

By the time the next bus comes he has still not come down the hill. This time I get on the bus, ending the possibility that I will know what Koto thought of Yad Vashem, a hand and a name. I want to know what he, a non-Jew, thought about the plight of the Jews—was this new information to him? Did he think of what went on in Japan, his own country, in the Pacific arena of the war?

As I ride from the suburbs of Jerusalem back into the busy central city, the bus fills up with more and more passengers, the traffic gets more dense, the closer we approach Jaffa Road. Stalled in the bus, I ask myself who among those I know would not stand idly by if a similar Holocaust happened today? I wonder if Koto had left the museum earlier than I, and feel comforted by the thought that he remained back on the museum grounds trying to help the trapped bird escape from the Hall of Remembrance, where it was caught somewhere behind the eternal flames.

❧

I am alone in Micha's house late on a Thursday night when I hear someone calling up from the street below. "Mee-cha, Mee-cha," a high-pitched birdlike voice chirps. "Mee-cha, Mee-cha, are you at home?"

I go to the living-room window, open it, stick my head out, and see the head of a man looking up as he begins to call "Mee-cha" yet again.

"Micha isn't at home," I tell him.

"Who are you?" he asks.

"A friend."

"May I come up?"

"I'll let you in," I say, knowing about the many visitors to

Micha's home. After Micha was interviewed on the radio answering questions from bewildered, and sometimes belligerent, people who did not understand how a Jew could be homosexual, many gay men have searched him out in the Old City.

"Ba-ruch," the man tells me his name as he passes by me into Micha's house. "I lost my keys in the playground," Baruch says, looking at me sheepishly and sucking his thumb.

"You mean the park?" I ask.

"You're one of us, too!" he responds, and quickly scampers up the stairs.

By the time I make it up to the living room Baruch has extended himself, full length on his side, head resting on his palm, on the sofa. I pull over a chair.

"I've known Mee-cha for-ev-er," he says, pronouncing Micha's name in the same birdlike way he used from the street, separating the syllables, giving each the same stress. He tells me that earlier tonight he had sex in the park with a border policeman, rolling his head and his eyes to emphasize certain details of his story. "When it was over I couldn't find my keys."

Baruch is a dark, thin, wiry man in his mid-thirties. Over the next hour, remaining in his reclining position on his side, he tells me his story nonstop, as if it were a monologue he performs regularly in a one-man play. The primary gesture he uses, and only during an occasional dramatic pause, is to suck on his thumb, as if it is from that digit on his left hand that he draws the sustenance he needs to continue.

"I came to Israel after Michael, my lover, died. I was only seventeen when I met him in Greece, where I'm from. I had spent two years as a flower child—yes, I was a flower child, imagine that—in San Francisco, but had enough summers of love by the end of the sixties so, tail between my legs, I came back to Greece, even though my parents were in Jerusalem." A pause and a thumb-suck. "Michael was no flower child. He was big, broad-shouldered, blond, and blue-eyed. He came to Greece before he was called up to serve in Vietnam." A pause and a thumb-suck. "He was my age. Gorgeous. Absolutely. Gorgeous. A bit taller than Ba-ruch. Very pornographic. Ve-ry." He shudders before taking another pause, another thumb-suck, this time adding a coy batting of his long dark lashes. "He would write me letters from A-sia." Another pause, a longer thumb-suck. "I still have the letters. And his me-dal. Ba-ruch has saved Michael's letters with Michael's me-dal, all these years.

"I was shell-shocked when he died, when he was killed, over there. I needed to see him again. I needed him. I flew to A-mer-i-ca for his funeral, to Rich-mond, Vir-gin-ia, where I stayed in his family's house, where Michael grew up." A pause, no thumb-suck. "The night of the funeral his older brother Reg-gie tried to bed me." A long thumb-suck and a fluttering of his lashes. "He looked so much like Michael, even more manly. So I let him. It was so confusing. After that I was faithful to Michael for three years. I never went back to Greece. I had no place to go so I came here to my family in Jerusalem. If all the creative Jews of the world came to live here in Israel what a nation it could be. Imagine." A deep sigh and a long pause. "I was faithful to Michael's memory for three years. But everyone needs a strong man next to him to fall asleep each night."

After these words Baruch kisses my hand, closes his eyes, and falls asleep with his thumb in his mouth. I do not move. I have never heard a story like his before. I feel very young, untainted. Despite all the physical and emotional pain I have felt, I have never felt as displaced as Baruch has felt these past fifteen years. I do not know whether it is tenderness or terror which keeps me here watching over him as he sleeps. I have never before met a man so wounded and, not yet twenty-four, I have no idea how many wounded men and women I will meet in the years ahead.

I am covering Baruch with a blanket when Micha returns.

"Ah, Baruch," he says when he sees his friend sleeping on the sofa. "He hasn't come around for a long time."

"He lost his keys," I say. "In the *playground*. He told me his entire story."

"His parents were Holocaust survivors," Micha tells me.

Baruch is not the only friend who comes to Micha's house unannounced during my visit to Israel. Besides Micha's younger sister, Rachael, who joins us every Shabbat and holiday, not many days go by without someone with some story appearing in Micha's living room. Or sometimes it is his neighbor, Beverly, and her muzzled dog, Buster, who visit.

It takes a while for Micha to explain the periodic early-morning phone calls that arouse him from his bed. For years, a rabbi from New York has called Micha for phone sex. "I met him through a friend when I was in New York, and we would just talk at first, but once he called me and I couldn't believe what was happening. How do you say no to a rabbi?"

Another man Micha knows from his trip to New York is in Jerusalem and I happen to be alone when he calls late in the afternoon.

"Micha's not at home," I tell him.

"Do you know when he is expected?"

"Not before dinner."

"You must be the friend who is staying with him."

"Uh-huh."

"I've heard a lot about you. I'll be over in fifteen minutes. I know where Micha lives." He hangs up before I get the chance to say another word.

Soon, the doorbell rings. I go downstairs to let the man in. This friend, Arnold, seems to be approaching sixty. He wears a knitted yarmulke on his bald head. When we sit down upstairs I could be sitting with one of my father's friends in Brooklyn. Not too far into our conversation of small talk Arnold puts his hand on my knee.

"I'll get you something to drink," I say, not knowing how else to escape his roving hand.

Before I can return from the kitchen with the lemonade I've poured, Arnold is behind me and when I turn around, defenseless with a full glass in each hand, he abruptly kisses me.

"Have you been to the Turkish baths?" he asks as if he did not do what he has just done.

"No," I manage to say, though I am clearly rattled.

"You're so beautiful," Arnold tells me. "How do men keep their hands off you? We should go together to the baths sometime."

After we drink lemonade I tell Arnold that I must go, that I need to go to the souk to get some items Micha will need for dinner. "I'll call you, I'm here a week," Arnold tells me before I close the door.

Over dinner, Micha tells me of his experience in the army when he was unable to throw a grenade. "It will make a man out of you," his commanding officer insisted.

"Did you do it?" I ask.

"I didn't want to. I had to," Micha tells me. "It is important to serve *eretz Yisrael*."

Later that night, more of Micha's friends arrive. Among them is the assistant conductor of the Israeli Philharmonic, who cannot believe I am happy being gay. "A homosexual who is loved by his father?" he says in disbelief after I tell him about my life back home.

"The two aren't mutually exclusive," I assure him, but refrain from telling him about the Jungian therapist who told me how gay men who have close relationships with their fathers have different problems with intimacy than other gay men.

The conductor, like many of Micha's friends, is married, has children. Without their families' knowledge, Micha's friends manage to see each other on the side.

Many of the gay men I meet at Micha's had first homosexual

experiences that were not pleasant. Avi was raped, Schlomo was groped at by monks at a monastery when he got lost on the Mount of Olives when a teenage boy. I am not yet aware enough to make any connection to my own history of unpleasant, even violent, sexual initiation.

❧

Everything that happens under the Middle Eastern sun happens in slow motion. I spend the next morning trying to read on Micha's roof. But the heat is enervating, makes reading impossible. As I doze, I imagine Shaoul's bronze skin getting darker as it absorbs the heat. I watch a bead of sweat begin to form above his left eyebrow, and then another, until his entire brow is filled with small jewels of perspiration, the same moisture I begin to notice between his thighs.

"Anybody home?" It is Shabtai, Micha's roommate, who I hear making his way up the stairs.

"There you are," he says, finding me on my lounge chair. "I went to visit my kid last night and stayed over there," Shabtai reports. "I took the day off and thought I'd show you some places you might not get to see on your own."

That night begins Shavuoth, the holy day that commemorates Moses' receiving the Torah on Mount Sinai. After returning from synagogue, Micha, who is an observant Jew, and David will read and study the Torah all night until dawn. How will they feel reading in Genesis God's commandment for men to be fruitful and multiply? Will they encounter "Man shall not lie down with man as he would with woman," the much quoted passage in Leviticus?

During dinner, Shabtai, who is not religious, invites me to spend the evening downstairs in his room while Micha and David study in the kitchen upstairs. "We'll be out of their way," he tells me.

Shabtai is fifty-two but looks more like thirty-five. He is balding slightly, has salt-and-pepper hair, and a beard and mustache to match. He is well over six feet, in terrific shape, has broad shoulders, hairy arms, a warm manner, and a friendly smile. His brown eyes can convey delight or reflect a deep brooding caused by what I imagine to be a painful past that causes conflicts that remain unreconciled.

I have been here a week and this is the first time I am in Shabtai's room. "Make yourself comfortable. There's no place to sit but on the bed. Do you like music?" Shabtai asks, bringing out a plastic instrument that looks like a recorder attached to a small organ keyboard. He begins to play, simply, the noted to "the Brindisi," the drinking song that begins Verdi's *La Traviata*.

Soon Shabtai offers me the instrument and I begin to play the same song before I segue into tunes I still remember how to play, transposing notes from the piano I played as a child.

I sit on the edge of the bed; Shabtai claps and hums along. As I play I begin to feel him caressing my thighs, then spreading my legs farther apart, his strong fingers in the creases on the side of, then under, my balls.

My breath begins to quicken as I am getting hard and I no longer have the breath to play any more music. I put the instrument down on the bed, lean back as he unbuckles my belt, unzippers and opens my pants, slides them down and takes my penis into his mouth.

As I lie back on the bed the conscious part of me seems to disappear. I am flattered, excited, that Shabtai is attracted to me, but I do not understand why. I cannot bring myself to ask him the questions I want to ask. What does he think of my body? What does he think of my legs? I am afraid of his answers. I become passive, inactive. The body wants what the mind cannot yet comprehend.

I search for his head with my hands, move my fingers through his thinning hair.

Then Shabtai takes off his pants, is on top of me, and I engulf his broad body in my arms as he rubs against me. When I focus on his body, my confusion dissolves. I reach down, slip down his briefs so I can knead his buttocks, firmly pulling him against me as he hastens the pace of his motions, grinds himself more forcefully, and finally lets out a deep, long groan of pleasure, then another, as he releases the tension caused by a long-held passion he has learned to endure.

After, I am relieved not only that it is over but that Shabtai does not need me to come. Still naked, he tells me he moved in with Micha after separating from his wife of over twenty years with whom he raised a daughter, now nineteen. He left them three months ago and he does not know if this is the right thing to do.

"You are so happy the way you are," he says. "Not conflicted like me and all the homosexuals here."

"What about Micha?" I ask.

"That's only the outside. He has his family here. I'm sure he wants children."

"But you have a daughter."

"And a wife. I hurt them. They don't understand. It isn't easy to reconcile. Either way I hurt myself, too."

As he tells me this his weathered face contorts with unexpressed emotion. He looks at me with the eyes of a confused teenager. Shabtai is the only married gay Israeli man I will meet who has had the courage to separate from his family. It has obviously not been easy for him, and I feel closer to him now that he has told me his story than when his body was on top of mine.

After sex, I am overwhelmed with conflicting emotions. I cannot tell whether or not Shabtai wants me to spend the night with him here in his room, and if he did I'm not sure that is what I want to do. Too afraid to ask or be asked to stay, not knowing what else to say or do, I kiss him good night and get up to go to my bed in Micha's room upstairs.

"You are very beautiful," Shabtai tells me from his bed.

"So are you," I answer at the door.

"I wanted to make it with you ever since you got here."

I take a long breath.

"You don't believe me?"

Though I know he is telling the truth, how can I tell him that I do not believe him? After he has opened up to me I still feel unwilling, unable, to talk openly about my feelings about my deformed legs. I know the confusion and strong emotions that lie behind my seemingly confident manner. At this time, I still think reticence is best, so in answer to his question I just shrug my shoulders, close the door, and start upstairs.

As I reach the landing, where I can either turn right into the living room or left into Micha's room, I can hear Micha and David speaking Hebrew.

In bed I can still hear Micha and David reading out loud and discussing the Torah in the kitchen. As I listen, I wonder what I could find in the ancient books, among the ancient laws, that could help give peace to Shabtai, who sleeps directly below where David and Micha will spend the night gleaning what they can from the five books Moses delivered to the Jewish people at Mount Sinai. Tonight, is there anything in what Micha and David, and so many Jews all over Jerusalem, study that can help reconcile the conflict caused by loving differently than expected, or needing to love in two distinctly contradictory ways? How do you reconcile love and respect for another with love and respect of yourself?

By the time the clock tells me it is almost two a.m. I have yet to fall asleep. Then I hear it. At first the ancient tones are faint, but soon it sounds as if it is coming almost from right outside the window. I get out of bed and go to the small window. I open it. Sticking my head outside I identify the music's source as coming from the Temple Mount, from the minaret of Al Aksa Mosque. I can see the dome glistening gold in the reflected light of the almost full moon. The Islamic holy month of Ramadan has begun.

❧

When Beverly, Micha's neighbor, comes to his house she will not spend any time at the door, moving quickly up the stairs in order to avoid spending any length of time in the lower, oldest portion of the house. "I get such awful vibes down there," she explains to me. "That room. Torture happened in there during the Crusades," she assures me. Her dog, Buster, muzzled so he will not eat the poisoned scraps of food left for the cats from the Arab Quarter, not being able to bark, whimpers loudly, as if to emphasize that he knows his owner is telling the truth.

Beverly, a woman with frosted beauty-parlor hair, is in her mid-fifties. She is a wealthy American widow who immigrated to Israel after her husband died of cancer in 1970. "It was so unexpected," she tells me. Beverly joined the wave of American Jews drawn to Israel by the heady confidence inspired by the Israeli victory in the Six Day War. In Beverly's case it was also a way to escape the loss of her husband. Her husband's wealth would have enabled her to live a comfortable life on Long Island or some other suburb in Westchester or in Connecticut, but here in Israel, where inflation runs at over 250 percent a year, her dollars go even further. Soon after her husband died she had a nervous breakdown, and today she manages to get by on her daily doses of lithium.

Our goal today is to drive to the Israeli military-occupation headquarters near Bethlehem in order to secure a new permit for Faiz, her driver, who lives in the West Bank. Faiz has been

Beverly's driver since she emigrated to Israel and made aliyah fourteen years ago.

In Beverly's car we quickly pass through the suburbs of Jerusalem, which have been built surrounding the city and annexed by Israel even though they technically remain on the occupied land seized from Jordan in the Six Day War. On modern roads we drive on once barren hills, winding our way through new-looking built-up communities not unlike those found in more lush Marin County, outside San Francisco.

Soon we have left the city behind and are driving on a two-lane highway through empty, dry land. The earth here is parched, a light beige, and rocky. Shielding my eyes from the midday sun, I see in the distance what seem like large tents, and what could be the outline of a camel.

"Bedouins," Beverly tells me. "See that," she says, directing my attention to a pickup truck kicking up a lot of dust as it makes its bumpy way through the rocky land between the tent with the camel and the road on which we are driving. "They have pickups now. And some even have tent televisions that run on batteries."

I look out at the long horizon of land that we are passing on both sides of the car. My eyes quickly examine the large boulders that seem to be the region's most salient feature. It takes us fifteen more minutes to reach a village.

We drive through the old Arab village, where a few men with white caftans on their heads walk slowly. Some stop to talk with each other; others smoke alone. One man leads a lamb, which captures Buster's attention in the backseat of the car. We are then on a road lined with tour buses idling in the stifling heat, and pass a large group of tourists standing near the sign, in Hebrew, Arabic, and English, for Rachel's tomb, a site holy to both Jews and Muslims alike.

Not far from the tomb Beverly slows the car in front of a compound surrounded by high barbed-wire fences. A crowd of

Arab men swarms in front of the entrance gate, only moving out of our way as Beverly inches forward. She drives up to one of the soldiers who man the gate.

"I'm here to see the commander," Beverly tells the soldier.

"Drive on through," the soldier says, motioning to the soldier in the small booth to raise the gate, which opens, and Beverly drives on through.

"He didn't even ask for ID?" I say.

"The commander is a friend of mine. They'll have to stay out there all day long," she tells me, pointing back at the line of waiting Arab men. "The commander only sees them at his whim."

"What are they waiting for?" I ask.

"Permits. Like the one we need to get for Faiz. That's why I'm here. He came to wait outside the gate for days and still he would not be seen."

As I look back outside the gate, the line of waiting men reminds me of the crowded waiting room full of Dr. Milgram's patients; how, as soon as your name is called you forget that the wait, which seemed endless, ever took place. But here it seems that the wait can actually be endless if you do not have the connections Beverly seems to have.

Beverly parks the car and we get out. "Come on, Buster," she calls to her unsure dog. "Let him out," she tells me.

We enter a building not unlike my Brooklyn elementary school, all concrete and tile walls, formica floors, metal stairs. As we go up a flight, an Arab man moves to the side; his body flush against the wall, when he sees the dog. This parting as Buster approaches is repeated every time we pass an Arab on the stairs or in the long fluorescent-lit hall.

"It's Ramadan," Beverly says, explaining the Arabs' reaction to her dog. When I do not respond she tells me that during Ramadan Muslims fast during the day and are not supposed to touch any animals. I want to ask why, knowing this, she took Buster with us, but remain silent.

As we enter an office, a secretary gets up and greets Beverly as if she is a long-lost friend.

"Is he in?"

"Go right through," the secretary says as she extends her arm in front of an open door. Beverly and Buster go in to see the commander and as I listen to their friendly chatter I look at the travel posters, the only adornment on the walls. I sit down on a bench where I can still hear Beverly talking with the commander, thanking him for his assistance in a showy voice that is much too loud.

Beverly's mission is accomplished and I hear her tootalooing the commander, see her waving her fingers as she passes the secretary, out of the office into the hall. I follow the permit-waving Beverly and Buster down the stairs, passing three more Arab men who must dodge and squeeze themselves against the wall to avoid touching the muzzled dog.

On our way out of the compound we pass the same men, who still wait for an audience beyond the gate.

"Now we'll deliver this to Faiz," she tells me.

We drive out into the hills and stop by an olive tree in front of a small stone house that has an old rusting car in the yard. A slow-moving Arab in his early fifties meets her at the door. He has a thin graying mustache and short-cropped hair, and wears a white button-down shirt, short sleeved, and khaki trousers wound tight around his skinny waist by a black belt.

"Come meet Faiz," Beverly calls to me. "Leave Buster in the car."

I slam the door before the dog can escape from the backseat. He cocks his head to the side as if to plead, then gives up and lies down on the seat in the shade of the olive tree.

"My family has lived here for hundreds of years," Faiz tells me as we stand looking out to the nearby hills. "I'm having problems proving it to the authorities. The old Turkish system, not to mention the British, does not make it easy to prove one's family has owned the land. Beverly has helped me with research and we have documented the history of the ownership of my land."

"My knowing the military commander doesn't hurt his claim," Beverly finds it necessary to add.

Faiz nods his head not only to agree with Beverly, but as if to assure himself that he is secure here and all will end in his favor. "It's better now than under Jordan," he tells me, speaking slowly in a warm, steady voice that holds my attention. "We still carry Jordanian passports, in schools use books from Amman, and the water pipes are built by Hussein. But Jordan won't let the refugees out of the camps. Go see the camps. It can't go on much longer. Just let there be peace."

Driving back from Faiz's house I have more time to contemplate the empty land littered with boulders that we pass on our way back to Jerusalem. The afternoon sun seems to cause the dust to rise from the earth, which heaves upward ever so slightly toward the sky. There are no trees here. No shadows. I search the boulders as if in their fossilized crevices I could find an explanation of this barren land's fascination, its primal hold on two ancient cultures in conflict with each other for too many years.

Growing up, all I heard from my parents and their friends was how the Jews were right, the Arabs wrong. I would search newspapers for other opinions. But any statement I would make to inject history, complexity, into the conversation was met with my father telling me I did not know what it meant to be a Jew.

What meaning is there in inanimate land? My connection to it is as tenuous as my connection to the Israel that finds itself in conflict with the Palestinians.

Driving back to Jerusalem what I feel is not complacency,

not quite guilt. Looking at these rocks I think that _home_ is not necessarily _land_, _land_ not necessarily _home_. To have an identity must one have a home?

All I can find among these rocks is the assured impossibility of being able to find the roots of an identity for an entire people here in this shadeless land. Do those who search for reflection in white stone—why was I born as I am?—do so to no avail?

ॐ

Even though I have never met him before, I know the man in the faded yellow Puma T-shirt, shorts, and sandals across from me on line in the Jerusalem bus station is Matthew.

I do not know if our mutual friend Judi told him about my legs, something I always am not sure of. Even when I'm sent to a new temporary job I hold this uncertainty in mind and search for clues when I am first encountered.

"You must be Matthew," I say.

"How did you know it was me?" he asks in the voice I recognize from our two conversations over the phone.

Matthew, the same age as I, is a tall husky bearlike guy with curly black hair, the same color as his mustache and beard. He wears unstylish large glasses, has an open smile. "Judi described you well," I tell him. "I'm easier to find," I say, alluding to my legs.

"Judi didn't tell me," he responds.

It is late afternoon and we are taking the bus together to a town near Haifa where Matthew has parked his car. From there we will drive the short distance to the Arab village where Matthew has lived this past year as part of his service for Interns for Peace, an international group that fosters Arab-Israeli relations.

"Do you like your fellow interns?" I ask Matthew.

"A good group. I hung out with one in particular who left a few months ago."

One in particular. I turn the phrase over in my head.

"We became partners," he continues.

Partners? Were they lovers?

Through all our talk on the bus I try to discern but cannot be sure whether or not Matthew is telling me he is gay.

Matthew's village is an old Arab community between Haifa and the Galilee. As we drive on a dirt road up to the house where he lives, Matthew waves to the men who are walking to the side of the car. He stops to exchange a few Arabic words.

"That's my landlord," Matthew tells me as we continue on our way.

"What do they make of you here?"

"At first they didn't know what to make of me. By now most of the villagers, though still wary, are my friends."

"Don't you get lonely?"

"Especially since my partner left." *Partner* again. "I've made some good friends at the kibbutz nearby. I'll take you there tomorrow."

Arriving home, Matthew cooks fish for dinner. As we eat we exchange our basic personal histories. I tell him of my writing; he tells me that after his year as an Intern for Peace he will study to become a rabbi. I tell Matthew that I am gay.

"I assumed if you were staying with Micha."

"You know Micha?"

"I never met him but I heard him on the radio."

"I imagine it's not easy to be gay and a rabbi," I offer.

"I don't know how I'll deal with it if it comes to that."

Finally, I decide on trying a more direct approach. "Do you mean being a rabbi or being gay?" I ask him.

"I guess both," he answers.

By the time we finish dinner and our conversation, it is dark outside and we go into the room that is set up as a traditional

Arab salon: many rugs and pillows, low benches along the wall. Matthew lights an incense candle. "Make yourself comfortable. I'm going to take a shower," he says.

I prop myself on a bench with pillows and while Matthew showers I flip through some Israeli magazines and Interns for Peace newsletters I find on a small table in the corner. I think about how both Micha and Matthew have a spiritual foundation more solid than mine. The importance of their being Jewish goes beyond the familiar rituals, the lighting of Shabbas candles, attending synagogue on Rosh Hashanah and Yom Kippur, reciting the blessings and lighting the menorah on Hanukkah. I feel somehow lessened, spiritually empty, in comparison to how these two men have fulfilled their need to believe.

My thoughts are interrupted by Matthew, still a bit wet, combing his hair as he stands in a towel before me.

"I'm exhausted," Matthew says. "I was hoping you'd sleep in my bed," he offers, looking directly at me.

"I was hoping you were going to ask," I answer as he bends down to take the incense candle with him into his room.

I follow him and in his room begin to take off my clothes. Matthew sits on the edge of the bed. Still wearing my pants I go over to him, run my fingers through his curly hair, outline the sides of his beard with my palms. As we begin to kiss I run my hands through the hair on his chest, nudge him gently back onto the bed. His towel drops to the floor.

"You're so comfortable making love with a man," Matthew whispers after we have finished making love for the first time.

"You're so comfortable being Jewish," I say.

Sometime during the long night—during our cycle of making love, talking, making love again—the by now familiar plaintive strains of Arabic prayer call from the minaret above the village's mosque. The ancient music blends with the sounds Matthew makes as I lick his body with my tongue, mixes with what I know to be my sighs as Matthew's tongue makes its way from the base of my neck, all the way down my spine past the crack of my ass to the base of my balls. Our sweat easily commingles with the fragrance of the incense, which escapes the room from the window left open to the hot night air.

It is not yet dawn and we are both lying on our backs when I ask Matthew what it is like for him to be homosexual in a small Arab village.

"You've seen the Arab boys," Matthew says. "We could walk arm in arm through the village without anyone raising an eyebrow, but if you were a woman, even if you were just a female friend from the States here for a visit, I could not spend the night with you here. The only other man I've ever slept with was my friend who was finishing his year here when I arrived. He finally got me into bed a week before he returned back home."

"Your partner?"

"Simon."

Diving back on top of Matthew I rest my head on his chest, stare through his thick black hair at his skin. All is silent now that the night of prayer is over. As I fall asleep I begin to dream the body on which I rest is the bricks of the destroyed temple's remaining wall. Matthew's skin is as white as the stones strewn over the land on the west bank of the Jordan River. As I search deeply into the body before me, I am, like Narcissus, looking for my reflection to be given back to me from the pool that ripples before my eyes.

But unlike the mythic figure I cannot discern a clear reflection in the pool in which I have been immersed since arriving in Israel. Like the reflections I saw as I lay on that cold metal table beneath the X-ray machine all those years ago, the vision remains incomplete, distorted as in the silver light that still hangs over the operating room guarding that part of me which for too long has remained, like the fragile body below, anesthetized.

All the questions that flood my mind when a man touches me, the questions that tonight dispersed, evaporated, like the sounds of Ramadan on the hot night air, once again pervade my mind.

When I wake I sense somewhere deep within me that part of me that has been dazed, that has remained asleep, inaccessible for all these years, is finally, in this ancient land, ever so slowly, beginning to stir, and I am excited by the danger, and very afraid.

❧

Even though Matthew invites me to spend Shabbat with him at the nearby kibbutz, I decide to stick to my plan and return to Jerusalem to spend Shabbat with Micha and his sister. After we eat lunch at the kibbutz, Matthew drives me to the bus.

As I am about to walk up the steps and onto the bus Matthew tells me he will call before I leave Israel. We hug. When I proceed onto the bus that will take me back to Jerusalem, I somehow know that even if I see Matthew again we will never recapture what happened last night. I begin to doubt that our one night together held much meaning for Matthew, who, like Adam, has yet to accept his homosexual desires. As the bus pulls away I see Matthew standing alone at the bus station and am saddened that what began for me last night in an Arab village so many miles from home will remain on hold, suspended until I find another man, different from Matthew, with whom to continue this necessary awakening of both body and soul.

❧

Back at Micha's, as I lie down on the bed and listen to the sound of heels on stone as shoppers bustle by on their way to the souk, I think about how back in the States, the rush-hour commute begins earlier on Friday, but not as early as here in Jerusalem, where workers are given the afternoon off, where streets are filled with Jews buying food in preparation for the Sabbath. Back in San Francisco all the bustle, the last remaining burst of that week's energy is spent getting to the earlier train or bus that will take us home. All that preweekend activity lacks the purposeful energy I have just absorbed by walking through the Old City.

My thoughts turn to holidays when I was young: the kiddush my parents would host in our apartment every year after services on the first day of Rosh Hashanah; my mother rushing home early from synagogue, missing the blowing of the shofar that would signal the end of the Yom Kippur fast so she had time to prepare and set out the meal we would be so eager to devour when the sun finally went down; and I remember a non-Jewish friend's birthday party during Passover, how I was the only youngster who had to bring his own snacks in a plastic bag, so I would have something to eat that was *kosher le Pesach*, untainted by yeast, no leavened bread, and thus allowed to be eaten during the holiday's eight days.

I know that in less than two hours I will be sitting in the kitchen across from Micha and Rachael. The Sabbath candles, just lit, will be, along with the challah, in the middle of the table. Before we eat, Micha's deep voice will softly sing the song that welcomes the Sabbath angel. As I drift off to sleep I follow the angel's flight into Jerusalem, where it flies above the bustling Jews in the streets below. From where it begins its flight I do not know.

❧

Tel Aviv is unlike Jerusalem. The atmosphere is less intense, more secular, cosmopolitan. Orthodox Jews dressed in their

black garb are rarely seen. Riding a bus down Dizengoff—past
the lunchtime crowds of workers, the busy department stores,
the modern apartment complexes—is like being in most large
cities around the world.

I am on my way to the House of the Diaspora, a museum in a
Tel Aviv suburb that chronicles the history and cultures of the
Jewish Diaspora. The museum is located on the campus of Tel
Aviv University. A large lawn, which is being watered by sprinklers, surrounds the entrance. As I walk on the path I notice off
to my right, in the center of the lawn near the sprinklers, the
figure of a man gesturing at me.

As I walk closer I see the man is an Arab whose uniform
identifies him as a groundsman who is watering the lawn. This
man is now on his knees, his arm extended toward the sky.
Then he prostrates himself on the ground, once again extending
his arms upward. Before he prostrates himself again he points
toward me, then toward the sky.

It is then I realize that this man wants me to know he is
praying for me. As I gesture my thanks back to him across the
lawn, I laugh to myself, remembering how during my stay in
England I would meet women in small towns on Sundays who,
on their way to church, told me they would pray for me as they
passed me by. What will they pray for? I always wondered.

In New York the street people I pass will usually greet me
with familiarity, as if being disabled makes me one of them.
When with a nondisabled friend these encounters embarrass
me by calling attention to my physical difference. I am annoyed
by not being able to walk down the street without interruption.

But when I am alone, like today, I am interested, if also a
little disturbed by these encounters. Is it a bond these men and
women feel? Or are they comforted by seeing someone they
perceive as more marginalized, more physically at risk, more
dependent than they are? Homeless veterans assume that my

legs were shot off in a war. How can I tell them one of the advantages of being disabled is not being asked to serve?

At times like this, even though I lead a far more secure and privileged life than theirs, I feel an odd connection with the homeless, whose situation, like mine, raises fears and questions that are camouflaged by attitudes of pity or ignorance from those whose lives are rooted in firmer ground. But perhaps it isn't the embarrassment that is most disturbing about these encounters. Rational or not, I live with the fear there might be a time when, not being physically able to support myself or to live on what the government decides to dole out, I, too, will end up living on the streets of a familiar city.

∾

I spend the rest of the day in the museum, following the various paths the Jews took when driven from their promised homeland. I walk from room to room, from displaced culture to displaced culture, studying maps, ritual objects. I walk through the built-to-scale replica of a wooden Polish synagogue burned by the Nazis, gaze up at the ornate ceiling from a Russian synagogue destroyed in a pogrom.

In another room I learn about a group of Marrano Jews who, during the Inquisition, sailed from Spain, landing first in Friesland in the Netherlands before moving south into Germany, and on to what is now Poland and Austria. Not knowing the true roots of the paternal side of my family (my mother's side I know came from Russia), I begin to spin a tale that explains my being mistaken for Puerto Rican, for being spoken to in Spanish in the hospital when I was young. Taking a break in the cafeteria, I take out the school photo, taken when I was in third grade, which I carry in my wallet and stare at my young face, imagining it derives from one of the families who escaped by boat from Spain.

For all of Jewish culture's emphasis on family I do not know much about my grandparents, their parents, or even my own parents. When, for a school project when I was in fifth grade, I asked my paternal grandmother to tell me about her trip on a ship to America when she was eight years old, all she said was: "They told me the roads were paved with gold. They weren't and I've been disappointed ever since."

∼

A blue Toyota waiting at the corner honks as Micha and I come out of a café. Micha opens the car door and moves the seat forward so I can hop in the back.

"Shalom, shalom," he says to the driver, who I assume is Dani Bender. "It is good to see you."

Dani Bender is a sabra, a native-born Israeli, whom Micha has known for many years. Micha did not mention Dani to me until the third week of my stay, which is surprising considering that Dani, like me, is a Jewish gay disabled man. "You probably want to meet my friend Dani," Micha told me in his understated way only a few days ago.

Micha and Dani, who Micha has told me is fluent in English, immediately are speaking Hebrew, and although I can understand a word every now and then, they speak too rapidly for me to fully understand.

"We are going to Jaffa," Micha tells me as he turns to face me in the backseat of the car. "They have good food there."

As Dani drives us to Jaffa, the old Arab town on the Mediterranean slightly south of Tel Aviv, I look at the hand controls that Dani uses to drive. They look more modern, more durable, than mine.

"What kind of hand controls are they?" I say to Dani from my backseat. When there is no response Micha looks at me, shrugs his shoulders, and begins to translate my question for Dani into Hebrew.

"The ones the government pays for," is Micha's translation of Dani's Hebrew response.

I begin to tell the story of how my out-of-date hand controls once broke while I was driving, how I could not stop my car when I reached a red light at a major intersection and had to veer my car around the oncoming cars until I was through the intersection and could safely stop along a curb.

When we get to Jaffa, Dani parks the car on the sidewalk in an alley. He places the placard in his windshield, not unlike the one I use in California, to show the car can park here because it belongs to someone who is disabled.

When we get out of the car I get my first full look at Dani Bender. In his mid-thirties, he is five foot seven, wears thick-rimmed glasses, which mask his bright blue eyes. His jaw is Germanic, his shoulders very broad, his arms quite muscular. His skin is pale, unlike most Israelis. He maneuvers himself out into the uneven street using his metal crutches, which have wrist cuffs that cover halfway to the elbow up his arm. As we walk I notice that although he can slowly walk with the use of his crutch-assisted arms, his thin legs do not bend. His method of walking reminds me of the teenage Israeli girl I met while we both waited in Dr. Milgram's office. "That girl came all the way from Israel for her polio," my mother would tell my father on our way back to Brooklyn.

During dinner, Middle Eastern–flavored meats, Greek salad, and pita bread, which we eat outdoors, Micha still serves as interpreter as I exchange life stories with Dani Bender. As he tells me of his trip to India, Dani begins to look directly at me, not Micha, even though he is still speaking Hebrew.

"You're the first Jewish gay disabled man I've ever met," I tell him as we eat sweet gooey baklava. "I'm surprised in a country with so many wars I haven't seen any disabled men in Israel."

"They stay at home," are the first English words Dani speaks. "There's nothing for them to do."

"How did you meet Micha?" I ask.

Dani begins to tell me he works as an international telephone operator and used to place calls for Micha. "I don't know many men who are homosexual," Dani admits. "He asked me out to lunch."

Back in the car, Dani invites me to return to Tel Aviv. "I work nights," he tells me. "We can spend an afternoon together."

On the bus back to Jerusalem I ask Micha if he has ever had sex with Dani.

"No, no, Dani never would," he tells me. "He usually does it with men he doesn't know. I can't believe he invited you back to Tel Aviv. I think he likes you."

❧

Two days later, back on the bus from Jerusalem to Tel Aviv, looking forward to seeing Dani, I think about Marilyn Golden, my only disabled friend. Marilyn, a Texan Jew and disability-rights activist, was my first peer-counseling teacher when I moved to San Francisco almost a year ago.

It was in Marilyn's class that I began my very tentative exploration of the long-dormant emotions concerning my disabled body. It was with Marilyn with whom I would finally be able to verbalize some of the questions I had long held silent in my mind. It was Marilyn who provided the perspective, the safety, and the understanding I needed to start peeling away the layers of oppression I had internalized and to dismantle the barriers I had unconsciously built in order to defend against the harmful attitudes, the disarming stares, that I am still only beginning to understand.

When the bus heads into the outdoor station I can see Dani waiting for me in his blue Toyota.

"Let's go to the zoo," he says when I settle into his car.

"The zoo?"

"It's a safari park."

"The one with the animals mentioned in the Bible?"

"Yes. That's the one."

On our way to the safari park I ask Dani how he managed to travel in India.

"Slowly. Very slowly," is his response.

We are at the entrance to the park and he rolls down his window to pay the entrance fee. "The day's on me," Dani informs me as he pays the guard. "Make sure the windows are closed," he says, echoing the warning posted on all the signs as we proceed into the drive-through zoo.

In the distance I see a group of animals gracefully running across the wide-open field. But they are too far away for me to see what kind of antelope they are. We drive farther but there are no animals.

"Must be the heat keeping them away," Dani says.

We go to the part of the zoo where you are allowed to walk around and Dani buys us some lunch at a food stand overlooking a stagnant pond. As we eat our burgers and french fries, we watch small white goats roam nearby.

There are a few young children surrounding the baby goats. As we approach, I hope they do not notice me and start pointing. I'm not sure how Dani will react to the way children usually react to my disabled legs. In the time we have been together I have noticed that although he walks with crutches his legs do not call the same kind of attention to him as mine do, as if the crutches serve as a satisfying explanation for the different way he walks.

When we get near the goats the children are too busy to notice us, but one of the goats comes over. As the goat ambles closer I notice he is limping. So does Dani. We laugh as we pet the disabled goat.

Later, we sit in Dani's car overlooking the perfectly blue Mediterranean. For as far as I can see the beach below is empty.

"Do you have a lover?" I ask.

"I did but it didn't work out," he says as he pulls on the lever that will make his seat recline.

"What happened?"

"I'm not sure but when we tried to live together after a few months it blew up. We were too different. I'm not sure he ever could have understood my body. My legs have no muscle left. I never let men see my legs. I drape a towel over them when I get into bed. It's not easy for two men who want to love each other here. And I'm not pretty with the polio. I was too insecure. I don't know."

The tide has picked up and the water, topped with white foam as it begins to break into waves, lashes the shore.

"I never will fall in love again," Dani tells me after a long pause. "I don't want to. It is too difficult for me."

I stare at the water. When I turn and look at Dani he seems to have fallen asleep.

As I look at Dani I search within myself for the familiar stirrings of attraction and find none of the uncomfortable tightness in my chest, no rapid breathing, that would lead me to reach out, touch his face, place his hand in mine. The car seat between us seems to have elongated from the heat of the afternoon sun and Dani seems to be as far away as the animals we could not see up close in the zoo.

I remember staying after class to have one-on-one counseling sessions with Marilyn, how she would draw attention to my legs. When she touched them, I would sweat and begin to tremble.

When Dani wakes I want to ask him what he thinks he would feel if he let a man who loved him see his withered legs, what he would feel if he let a man he loves touch him there. I want to tell him about Charlie, the Harvard graduate I met last year in San Francisco, who after three months of sleeping together never touched my legs, how I was never able to ask him, or any man with whom I have been naked, if he thought my legs, so twisted, so scarred, were attractive, or believe them if they said they were.

But I do not yet know the words with which to ask Dani these questions. Nor do I have the courage to face asking them of myself. I am afraid to cause us both discomfort and instead become distracted by the sun, now lower in the sky, reflecting off of one of Dani's crutches resting at his side. The light forces me to squint, but no matter which way I turn it is too difficult to open my eyes fully.

I open the car door and, shielding my eyes from the sun, walk to the edge of the cliff, where I am able to see the lone man who now walks on the beach, at the edge where the water reaches for land.

I lie down on my side and using my palms as a pillow fall asleep and begin to dream about the terrorists who were recently caught in a boat as they were trying to come to shore.

When I wake I cannot tell how much time has passed. Dani is now standing near me. He has removed his T-shirt and is changing into a light blue dress shirt that matches the color of his eyes.

"All the sun will make me tired at work tonight," he says as I look admiringly at his muscular upper body, developed from the task of pulling his atrophied legs around for so many years. I could easily reach out and pull him toward me but as if he senses what I am thinking he shyly finishes buttoning up his shirt more quickly, and moves out of my reach toward the car.

"I find men at the bus station," Dani tells me as he drives me to Habimah, where Micha will join me at the theater. "Sitting in the car they do not know about my legs. I know the dark streets where I never have to get out of the car, just need to open the door enough. When it's over I drive off. It's easier that way."

As we reach the city, I cannot shake off the ineffable sadness that I seem to have absorbed by watching Dani asleep in the car. Nor can I forget the sight of him, shirtless, when I woke on the promontory cliff above the Mediterranean Sea.

"Thanks for taking me there," I say as we maneuver through downtown traffic. Dani does not take his eyes off the road. He smiles.

Later that night, even when watching the play, I cannot stop from returning to that moment in Dani's car.

What would have happened if I followed through and started making love to him? What would have been Dani's reaction when, after undressing him, I revealed his stricken limbs? And if he acquiesced what would I have felt making love to another disabled man?

If I could ever answer these questions I know more questions would take their place. Perhaps it is this seemingly infinite sequence of questions that swells up like the high tide of the pristine Mediterranean water, clouding its clear surface, that prevented me from touching Dani in the car that afternoon, from toppling him on top of me as I lay so high above the water.

As endless as each person's search for acceptance is the body's search for beauty. Like the ocean's water constantly being pulled to shore, the body is then pulled away, yet again, by an unseen force you know only by getting close to it, immersing yourself in it, always being careful not to go out so far that you are pulled helplessly along.

Late that night I am quiet on the ride back to Jerusalem. Despite having been with men with whom I have made passionate love, men who I could not deny were attracted to me, even after Adam in London, and Matthew just a week ago here in Israel, I still wonder what it will take—my being attracted to another disabled man?—to let myself be pulled farther out, closer to understanding, to know I will not drown, but be returned safely back to shore.

~

No matter where you are in Israel, a man who wants to meet a man need look no farther than Gan Ha'atzmaut, Independence Park, a version of which is found in every city or town.

In Jerusalem, Independence Park is easy to find. Just outside the Old City walls, not far from the King David Hotel, down the street which still looks like the no-man's-land it was before the 1967 war, you reach an entrance to the park. In this corner is the ancient Arab cemetery. Among these tombs, at night, men search for men. But during the day, the area beyond the playground is the prime cruising ground.

Back in the States I never cruised a park for men. Since Adam, I have met men predominantly in bars. I was once denied entrance to a gay bar in Florence, Italy, because I was disabled. "No belong here," the handsome man in charge told me after I explained to him in no uncertain terms that I was gay and I belonged inside.

Thus far, not once has a sexual encounter with a man I met at a bar led to anything more important than a one-night stand. Sex has never led me to a deeper exploration of my identity as a gay disabled man. On the contrary, because my disability is never mentioned, because during these sexual encounters men do not touch my legs, except for this crucial absence, it is as if I pass, as if I am not disabled after all.

The park is empty during the hottest part of the day. I am sitting on a bench when I notice Shaoul, dressed in his waiter's uniform. I haven't seen him since the day after my arrival. When I see him his first response is to look away, but then he walks over.

"I'm on my way to work," he says sheepishly, as if he is embarrassed that I have met him here.

"Do you come here often?" I ask.

"There should be no talking before sex," he replies. "I've got to be getting on."

As Shaoul turns to go, I see a very dark man walking on the path toward me. With the comparison readily at hand, this man looks like an even darker, more attractive version of Shaoul.

"Tell Drew I'll call him before I leave," I say.

Shaoul looks at me when I mention Drew's name. He is about to say something—not to tell Drew I met him here?—but thinks better of it and goes on his way. As he passes the even darker man they stop for a minute to talk amiably as if they know each other.

Then this man surprises me by sitting next to me. He tells me his name is Ya'acov. He is from Iran.

"You're American, right?" he asks.

"You're the first person who hasn't mistaken me for Israeli," I tell him. Up close I see everything about Ya'acov is dark—his hair, his skin, his eyes. "How do you know Shaoul?"

"I see him in the park."

During our conversation Ya'acov places his hand on my shoulder. As we speak he moves his hand to my chin, down to the hollow of my chest. He takes the T-shirt out of my pants and entwines a finger around a hair on my stomach. Then, to my surprise, he puts his hand down my pants and starts rubbing my crotch. I cannot believe it is midafternoon and I am sitting on a park bench in Jerusalem with this beautiful Iranian man's hand down the front of my pants.

"Feel good?" he asks.

"Not here," I reply. Knowing Micha will not be home this afternoon I tell Ya'acov we can go back to where I am staying.

"I have not much time. I have to go to work."

"I'll pay for a taxi." As I get up I tuck my T-shirt back in my pants.

We are silent until we reach the house. "I've been here before," Ya'acov tells me. Upstairs, I watch him strip off his clothes, unveiling his dark brown skin. He slips off his underwear and is too quickly on top of me, kissing me, parting my lips with his tongue, grinding his groin into mine.

He pulls off my clothes as he continues to explore my mouth with his tongue. Overwhelmed, like I was with Shabtai, I do not know how to react to his passion. I stare at him as if I am trying to come to terms with the elusiveness of his beauty, searching for clues to how someone so beautiful might feel.

He sits up and as he strokes himself his fingers twist my nipples, causing twinges of pain. Still, despite his insistence, I am passive, my desire dormant.

Then he slaps me.

"What are you doing?"

"I'm trying to wake you up."

"Don't do that again."

"I want you to fuck me."

"Okay," I say, not letting on I have never fucked a man before.

"How do you want to fuck me?"

"Bend over the edge of the bed," I hear myself say.

A moment later Ya'acov is in this position I have fantasized. The sight of his ass, delicately outlined with dark black hair, arouses me like I have never been aroused before. I have always wanted to have a man in this way but up until now the opportunity never presented itself. For this I have come to Jerusalem?

I enter Ya'acov and begin fucking him, at first slowly, then with an abandon I did not know I was capable of.

I watch as I enter, pull back, and enter him again, and again, thrusting harder and harder until I no longer know where or who I am, no longer know who the man is I clutch on to beneath me, forget I even have a body—but what if not my body lifts me to the height I am reaching now?

I hear Ya'acov moan louder, feel his body rise, tense up, and fall back to the bed. But I am not ready yet. I thrust harder, deeper, harder, deeper, one more time until I feel myself ejaculating into the most beautiful man I have been allowed to touch, holding on to the most desirous man who has ever spread his body prostrate before me.

No sooner than I have pulled out of him, Ya'acov has dressed himself again. "Tell Micha I say hello," he tells me, then kisses me good-bye.

As I stare at the ceiling I can only wait until I reenter my body. I remain naked, heart still racing, totally spent on the bed, wondering if Ya'acov and Shaoul have ever had sex, whether or not Ya'acov is married.

∾

I spend my last day in Jerusalem exploring the Mount of Olives, beyond the Temple Mount, outside the Old City walls. Micha accompanies me to the Jewish cemetery, where visitors do not leave flowers, but white stones. He takes me to the Garden of Gethsemane, where Jesus was arrested after being betrayed by Judas.

"Look at this," Micha calls from a grove of ancient olive trees.

When I catch up with him he stands beneath a sign that tells us this is where Christ was arrested.

"Now, look at this," Micha says, pointing at another sign across the path. This sign, in a fancier, more Gothic script, makes the same claim as the first sign.

"Two different sects," Micha informs me. "Each believes it happened in a different place."

We continue up the mount until we have a clear view of the Old City.

"That closed-up portion of the city wall is the Golden Gate, where the Messiah will enter the city when he returns."

During my stay in Israel I have learned that the idea of the Messiah not only separates Jews from Christians, but causes conflict within Judaism itself. I have heard Zalman Schachter, a New Age rabbi from the States, lecture about how the Messiah is not a being, but represents the better part of each individual and that by acting upon that better part each of us works toward the return of the Messiah. I have been told about the ultra-Orthodox religious sects, the black hats, descendents of the Jews from Borough Park, themselves descendants from eighteenth-century sects in Romania, Russia, Poland, and Hungary, who in their Brooklyn apartments listened to the radio during World War II, thinking it was only a matter of days before the Messiah would return to end their people's suffering.

These Jews, most of whom came from displacement camps, others more recent settlers from Brooklyn, now live in Jerusalem in an area known as Mea She'arim, which looks as if it is a nineteenth-century Eastern European shtetl, do not give credence to the existence of the State of Israel, since, according to their belief, the Jewish Kingdom cannot reconsolidate itself until after the Messiah has arrived. They follow no civil, only religious, laws.

Up on the Mount of Olives it is another clear hot day. Looking out at the city that has become his adopted home, Micha begins to talk about the crossroads he is reaching in his life. "I am the first son born to my parents after the Holocaust. They expect certain things of me. As hard as I try I still can't reconcile being both Jewish and gay," he confesses. "I try to be an observant Jew, at the same time being out and helping the gays I meet. But to be a Jew you must have children and no matter how I rationalize my desires, that remains a desire for me, too."

As I look out over Jerusalem, past the Dome of the Rock, glittering as usual in the midday sun, I try to find the roof of Micha's house, one street south and one street west of the Temple's remaining wall.

"You live so close to the Wall," I hear myself say. "That must be some sign from God."

As I continue looking over the city, despite all the political and social tension, resting peacefully, secure within its walls, I know that in a day's time this trip will begin to filter through my mind, becoming memory. As I continue to stare into the glare of the heat rising from the white stone below, I am transfixed by what I see before me. There, at the Golden Gate, blocked up for hundreds of years, the sun hits the stone at such an angle that light is reflected back and I must shield my eyes.

All of a sudden, a billowy cloud, out of nowhere, but from the direction of Jordan, behind us, dims the sunlight, causing a shadow to fall upon the Golden Gate. It is as if, for that moment, an invisible hand has touched the Gate, and I imagine that climbing down to examine it, I will see an indentation in the stone—slight but there. On my last day in Jerusalem, I leave the Mount of Olives knowing that the Gate has been pushed open, ever so slightly, making it that much easier for the Messiah, whether an actual person or not, to enter into the city, perhaps unnoticed, but never to those who believe, unknown.

❧

At the end of a long period of travel, perception begins to blur. Senses that were once heightened by the eagerness to experience the new, the unknown, begin to flag as your body prepares to return to its more familiar home.

My last night in Jerusalem, after packing, I confirm tomorrow's flight, then go out with Ofra, Micha's Yemeni friend. Ofra is one of the most beautiful women I have ever met. She is tall, with thickly flowing black hair, dark lively eyes, tanned skin. As soon as we met, a few Shabbats ago, I knew she was in love with Micha.

Ofra and I walk south, past Mount Zion to Yemin Moshe, Jerusalem's first suburb outside the city walls, built by Moses Montefiore, an English Jew, in 1857. In Yemin Moshe, which houses Mishkenot Sha'anim, a world-renowned artists' residence, the buildings are Victorian, the cobblestoned streets lined by streetlamps, the inhabitants very well-to-do. We pass where Montefiore's carriage is displayed. Above, on a hill, Montefiore's windmill, the top blown off by the British to hinder the area's defense by Jews during the siege of Jerusalem, remains still even on this cool, windy night.

As we stroll Ofra tells me of her concern for Micha.

"What future is there for him?" she asks. Although Ofra knows that Micha is gay she is unable to come to terms with his sexuality and what that means to her relationship with him.

I know I should be more blunt with her, but it has been a long trip and I am tired of playing the role of the happy homosexual. "He'll find his way," is all I can muster the energy to say.

"And what of you?" she asks. Looking at this beautiful woman standing next to me I know that in another life I, like Micha, would fall in love with a woman just like her. Now, here, all I can do is shrug my shoulders and smile.

We stand at the edge of Yemin Moshe, looking past Mount Zion to the Old City, its stone walls floodlit, across from us. At night, lit up like this, Jerusalem seems somewhat fake, surreal. The light casts a yellowish tint upon the stone.

As we walk back within the walls I am left with one final image of my trip to Israel, an image that makes me, for a moment, consider a life I imagine would be much easier, a life

I know I cannot lead: Ofra's dark hair blowing wildly in the wind.

∾

Early the next morning Micha accompanies me to the station, where I will catch the bus to Ben Gurion Airport. I make it to the airport with plenty of time to make my way, once again, through security.

Airborne, I take out the translation of my bar mitzvah haftorah Micha worked on for me during my stay. I unfold the paper and read. It begins:

Where is the house that you may build for me?
And where is the place that may be my resting place?

Heading back, first to New York, then to San Francisco, I am haunted by these questions, lines I sang to an ancient tune before my friends and family who sat listening in the congregation. As I repeat these lines in Hebrew the tune comes back to me but as I begin to fall asleep they are transformed into the chanting of Ramadan, so familiar during my stay in the Holy Land.

When I wake I watch from the small airplane window as the light in the sky begins to wane. I do not know how long I was asleep. I am unaware of what we are flying over, unsure of what waits for me after I land.

Not yet twenty-four, I am not sure what I have seen in Israel will mean to me in the years ahead. I do not know that when my parents finally make their trip to Israel, they will not be able to walk safely in any quarter in the Old City of Jerusalem. I do not know they will not be able to visit where I visited on the West Bank. I do not yet know the Arabic word *intifada*.

I do not know that over seven years later I will meet Kamal

Boullata, a Palestinian visual artist who found himself traveling
abroad during the Six Day War and was not allowed to return
to his home in East Jerusalem since during his absence that part
of the city had become part of the Land of Israel. Meeting
Kamal will personalize the Palestinian-Israeli conflict, clari-
fying the situation beyond the skewed headlines.

Kamal will show me a film in which I will see him talking to
an Israeli bureaucrat, who in a Kafkaesque sequence tells him
why he cannot receive automatic citizenship like any Jew any-
where in the world. His application will have to wait and even
then it is doubtful Kamal would receive the citizenship he
desires. I do not know when I watch this film I will think about
my own encounters with the byzantine Social Security forms
and laws concerning disability in my own country. Sitting on
the plane I do not know that despite the difference between
Kamal's situation and my own, both of us, to varying degrees,
are treated as second-class citizens in our own homes because
our identity—who we are—is not understood independent of
the dominant culture in charge.

As I fly home I do not know that Kamal will show me his
vividly colored paintings inspired by the gates of Jerusalem, the
very gates I viewed from the Mount of Olives my last day in
Israel over seven years before, and that I will feel a common
bond with my new friend and know the current situation is
untenable and must somehow end with both a Palestinian
homeland and an Israel that remains secure.

On that El Al flight what I do know is that changes have
begun to take root within me during my stay in Israel. My time
with Micha, with Matthew, with Dani, and my experiencing
and witnessing the lives of gay men in a country that is not
my own, have planted seeds of awareness about my identity
as a Jewish gay disabled man that will blossom in ways still
unknown when I return.

Unknown to all of us rushing toward our destination in this

narrow room of protected air, are the fates awaiting each and every one of us, as well as the fate of disputed land. I do not know how Micha will resolve his conflicting needs, nor if I will see Matthew again. I do not know that six months later in a bar in Greenwich Village I will meet Jason, who does not know about the virus that reproduces in his bloodstream. I do not know he will move back with me to San Francisco and that after five years of living together I will leave him for another man, and my relationship with that man, together with the physical problems my disability will cause, will precipitate a crisis in which I will be forced to come to terms with all that my body remembers.

Landing in New York I do not know any of this. I do not feel even a trace of the pain I will feel daily in my back five years later, the pain that will force me to change the patterns of my life. I am buoyantly expectant as I make my way through customs, retrieve my backpack, and begin my adjustment to returning home.

THREE

Wishing for the Cloths of Heaven

My emotions are inappropriate for my size.

—LOUISE BOURGEOIS

*Y*EARS ago, toward the end of my bath, I called for my father. He entered the bathroom and knelt beside the tub. When I lifted my feet from the water, my father took the bar of soap, wet it, and as I rested my feet in his palm he gently slid the soap over my skin and between my toes.

Tonight, taking a bath, I do not submerge my head in the water to listen to my parents' voices as I did when I was young. I do not call for my father when I am ready for him to bathe my feet and legs.

Instead I close my eyes and conjure my father's hands on my scars. But no matter how hard I try, the sensation of my father's caressing hands cannot be called from memory. Like those distorted reflections given back to me years ago by the X-ray machine above my naked body, it is as if my legs, which minutes ago brought me to the tub, remain anesthetized, rendered inaccessible except for utilitarian tasks, or an occasional sudden jolt of pain.

With my eyes still closed, I rest farther back in the tub, feel the cooling water just above my neck, that place where so much of physical memory seems to be stored. It is now, my body submerged in water, that they, one by one, a succession of lovers, enter the room. They, like my father, kneel beside the tub and begin, one after the other, to bathe my tired feet and legs.

At first, I want to open my eyes. I want to stop myself from experiencing my lovers' hands on my scars. But I do not open my eyes. Nor do I escape from the discomfort rising up my spine by asking them what it is they feel when they touch me.

I keep my eyes closed until I can bear it no longer. Peering over the edge of the tub I assure myself that, tonight, no one is in the room with me. I lift my hand from the tub and touch the cold tiled floor.

∾

Alone in an unfamiliar room, I turn on the light and reach for the book beside my bed. During the past month, no matter what time I have gotten into bed, I have known that eventually, whether it be one, two, three, or four hours later, I will wake up. I will be sweating, my heart and mind will race, I will be unable to breathe.

But tonight, I turn to the familiar page and read:

Had I the heavens' embroidered cloths,
Enwrought with golden and silver light
The blue and the dim and the dark cloths
Of night and light and the half-light,
I would spread the cloths under your feet:
But I, being poor, have only my dreams;
I have spread my dreams under your feet;
Tread softly because you tread on my dreams.

I read this poem, first to myself, then softly aloud, again and again until I have memorized the lines and can safely place the book next to me on the narrow bed. I continue to repeat the poem over and over until its lines replace the scene of when I am passed from stranger's hand to stranger's hand, the soothing meter of poetry overtakes that of Miguel fucking a twenty-year-old Dutch boy he met at the end of the summer, the voice of the poet drowns out my brother's voice telling me I will no longer grow.

Tonight, in this poem, "He Wishes for the Cloths of Heaven," written by William Butler Yeats almost a hundred years ago, I find the compassion I have been searching for and with the lines ending *cloths, light, cloths, light, feet, dreams, feet, dreams* plangent in my head, with the book resting comfortably at the side of my pillow, I am, finally, able to fall back to sleep.

In my dream I am startled by a bright light.

There is someone holding a large searchlight standing in my room.

"Who's there?" I shout.

"I didn't mean to startle you," a voice says, as the light is turned off.

My eyes adjust to the darkness. Not knowing what room this is I instinctively listen for sounds. The hum of a fan or a heater, distant footsteps, voices murmuring outside the door.

"We make rounds every night to check that everyone's okay," the voice, a woman's voice, tells me. "The rules."

I sit, head bent, on the edge of the bed, trying to control my rapid heartbeat. I think of taking a pill, but remember the night almost a month ago when, physically unable and afraid to be living alone, I needed one and could not remember what happened when I woke the next morning. If I know anything it is that I want to be able to remember.

❧

"It's policy," Dr. Riskin, my psychiatrist, tells me at our first meeting early the next morning.

Right away, Dr. Riskin reminds me of the young Elizabeth Taylor. I would have preferred Montgomery Clift, but I was not consulted.

"Policy?"

"To make sure the patient is still alive."

"What?"

"Suicide."

"Oh."

"Have you ever thought of killing yourself?"

I know that if I tell her yes I have thought of killing myself, she will believe me and the nurse will turn the searchlight on in my room, waking me up every night. But if I say no I will be lying.

"Of course I have," I tell Dr. Riskin. "But I wouldn't do it."

"What makes you so sure?"

"Look, I need to be able to tell you these things. I need to be able to express that level of despair. That's why I'm here."

"Why are you here?" she asks, looking through her notes.

Can't you find it in the file? I want to reply, but instead I outline the events that led to my checking myself into Beth Israel Hospital's psychiatric ward less than twenty-four hours ago.

❧

At the end of 1984, six months after I return from Israel, I am in New York to begin rehearsals for *A Human Equation*, my play about the triangular relationship of a bisexual poet, a gallery owner, and a graduate student who is writing his thesis on the poet, which will have a four-week run at LaMama. Just before rehearsals are to begin, the well-known experimental actress who is to play Lillian, the gallery owner, drops out because of illness. My director decides he cannot do the play without her, and, having already raised the money for the production, I reluctantly take over directing the play.

The night before rehearsals begin, I go to wind down in a bar. I notice a man who sits alone at a corner table, drinking a beer. Wearing jeans, a navy blue sport jacket, white shirt, and tie, he seems out of place, uneasy. He looks much younger than those who frequent this place. Though his dark eyes dart around, mostly they look at the floor. Out of the corner of his eye he sees me sitting on a stool at the bar.

Back then, in bars I would plant myself at a table or on a stool at the bar and stay in one place as long as possible. When I saw someone I would like to get to know, I would stay put. And even when I had to go to the bathroom I would put it off for as long as I could to avoid making my disability noticeable by standing up and walking. By deciding to remain stationary, I rarely met the men I wanted to meet, the men I was attracted to. Those I met would have to come over to me, or I would meet them by chance when they happened to take an empty seat near where I sat at a table or at the bar.

All of a sudden, the man I saw at the corner table is standing next to me. "Hello," he says, not looking at me but down at the floor. "I just came from the opera. It was *Elektra*," he tells me.

"I used to have a friend who ushered at the Met. He'd get me free tickets but when I'd go I'd fall asleep," I say.

"I'll have to take you," he declares. "I'm Jason. There's an empty table in the corner."

"I have to go to the bathroom," I say, unable to hold it in any longer. I hop off the stool and immediately turn away. As I walk to the bathroom I know Jason is watching me. I wonder if he is still interested in me, or whether he will be like the man I once met who, after talking the entire evening as he ran his fingers up and down the length of my arm, decided not to go home with me after I stood up and he discovered I was just over five feet tall.

Leaving the bathroom, I notice Jason is sitting alone, waiting for me at the corner table. If he is surprised at my legs he doesn't show it.

"That guy over there keeps bothering me," he tells me when

I join him. "I went home with him once and he won't leave me alone. I'm trying to be celibate."

"Celibate?" Is he just telling me this because he doesn't want to have sex with me?

"Close to three months now," Jason says, with a mixture of pride and impish delight reflected in his smile. "I'm learning to meditate. And I'm a vegetarian."

"How old are you?" I ask.

"Twenty-seven," he answers to my surprise.

Jason's eyes never meet mine as he tells me he is a painter and that he studied at the School of Visual Arts in Manhattan before leaving for Paris. Since returning to New York he's been working nights as a graphic artist, living with his parents on Long Island.

I tell Jason about my poems published earlier that year, about the impending rehearsals for my play, that I live in San Francisco.

As he tells me his coming-out story—how when he found a man with whom he fell in love, Jason lunged at him on the balcony of a harborside motel, almost toppling them both over the edge and into the water below—I am amused by how he over-dramatizes his story.

"When I told my mother I was bisexual," he tells me, "three months later she asked if I was bisexual where were the women?"

"I came out to my parents on the phone," I tell him. "When I asked them why they were silent my mother asked: 'What do you want us to do, jump out the window?'"

Soon, Jason is drunk and telling me when he was in college in upstate New York he once woke up drunk in a forest, thinking he had been raped earlier that night. He nonchalantly reports that he was once arrested for stealing furniture from a hotel that had just closed down. For a short time, he worked as a stripper.

I don't know whether Jason is telling me the truth, and if he is, whether there is more to these tales than he is letting on. Is he someone I want to have sex with? At least he has diverted my attention from my play.

When the bartender calls last call, Jason tells me he has to catch the last train home.

"You can stay where I'm staying," I tell him.

"I can't. Give me your number. I'll call you."

I want to ask if it's his trying to be celibate or my legs, but write down my number instead.

∽

The first week of rehearsals are exciting, but it's obvious the replacement actress is not up to the job. I am surprised when I receive a message that Jason called. On my day off I call him. His mother answers. I ask to speak to Jason.

"Craig, Craig, it's for you, Craig," I hear her call.

"I've got it, Mom," he says when he picks up another phone.

"It's Kenny," I tell him.

"I'm glad you called."

"Who's Craig?"

"That's my real name. I changed it when they couldn't pronounce Craig when I was in Greece. My family never has gotten used to my being Jason."

I invite him for dinner one night before he has to go to work.

"I wish you could stay," I tell him after we've eaten.

"We can have sex on New Year's Eve," he says.

"What about your celibacy?" I ask.

"My three months will be over then. Call me," he says before running down the stairs.

The next day I call him and his sister answers.

"Who's calling?" she asks.

"Kenny," I tell her.

"Oh, Craig thinks you're very special," she blurts out. "He's disappointed you live in San Francisco."

∾

I'm excited about the prospect of having sex with Jason on New Year's Eve. We plan to meet a friend of mine and take her to a party given by Jason's friend who lives on St. Mark's Place. At the party, Jason gets very drunk, constantly talks about how sexy our hostess's boyfriend is, and when it is time to leave tells me he wants to go out and drink some more.

"I thought we were going to have sex," I say.

"Next time," he says before kissing me for the first time.

The next day, an obviously hungover Jason calls to tell me he wants to spend next weekend with me. I tell him we can drive to my parents' small summer house upstate.

At the house, the first night, Jason seems reluctant to take off his clothes. When I get into bed, he is very quiet.

"What's the matter?"

"Nothing."

"You seem like you don't want to be here," I say.

It is then that Jason first tells me about his former lover, Eddie, with whom he lived in a baroquely decorated apartment in Jersey City for a few years. When their relationship was on the rocks, and in reaction to Jason's sleeping around, Eddie began seeing another man. Devastated by being abandoned by Eddie, Jason escaped to Paris, where he was kept by a rich Frenchman, while also having sex regularly with the son of a diplomat from Madagascar.

"This is the only time I haven't been drunk my first night with a man," he confesses.

I hear myself tell Jason very crucial things about myself, including the history of my legs, and as I tell him I realize my report is emotionless. I could be talking about someone else.

During the rehearsals of my play, it is obvious there are many problems with the actors. I spend sleepless nights listening to *Lohengrin*, a recording Jason bought me so I can prepare for our first opera together. "Pay attention to the passion, not the language," he told me.

The week before my play opens, when we move into the theater, technical problems abound. The night after the first dress rehearsal, Jason's night off, he takes me to see *Ariadne auf Naxos*, and his enthusiasm is contagious.

After, unable to sleep, I take a bath. The music of Ariadne's famous aria, in which she renounces love because her lover, Theseus, has abandoned her, rises to its ecstatic conclusion in my mind. To my surprise, Jason comes into the bathroom. He kneels by the tub and absentmindedly picks up a bar of soap and begins to wash my feet.

"Nobody has done this since my father bathed me," I whisper. Lying back in the tub I feel Jason's fingers slide up the scar on the side of my right leg. He touches the holes where the pins were inserted after surgery close to twenty years ago.

Soon, I am telling him the names my brother used to call me when I was young. Aside from my psychologists, Jason is the only person with whom I have shared these memories.

Even though there was a snowstorm that day, my play opens, and, despite the bad weather, everybody who has given money for the production shows up. Telegrams arrive from friends not in New York, including one from Matthew in Israel. When Ellen Stewart, the legendary founder of LaMama, comes on stage to welcome the audience, ringing her traditional bell before the play begins, I am in the back row of the sold-out theater, holding my breath, knowing the production is now out of my control.

At the party that follows, I introduce Jason to my parents.

"I was sitting behind you," he tells them. "It was like watching two plays."

Needing some distance from the disappointing production, I miss some performances and start to spend time with Jason at his parents' house on Long Island. One night we are downstairs in the basement that is his bedroom, listening to opera on his ancient stereo with awful sound, when Jason takes off his clothes, and mine, and tells me he wants me to fuck him.

Jason gets on top of me. I feel myself inside him and hear a young woman's voice yelling, "Craig, Craig," at the top of the stairs. The voice is followed by footsteps, getting louder as they approach. Jason seems lost in the physical sensations of the sex we are having.

"I think someone is coming," I tell Jason, and we both start laughing.

"Oh, my God, it's my sister," he says, jumping off of me and wrapping us both in the sheets.

"Am I interrupting?" his sister asks from the bottom of the stairs. "Mommy told me Kenny was here and I wanted to meet him."

"Hi," I say, smiling.

"I guess this isn't the right time," she says.

Again, Jason and I burst out laughing. This time his sister joins us, too.

That week, I decide not to go back into the city. I wait in Long Island for Jason to return from work on the last train. One night, alone in his room, I hear his mother and sister arguing vehemently upstairs. His mother's voice gets louder; his sister begins to cry.

When I get up the next morning, I leave Jason sleeping and go upstairs. On the kitchen table is a note to me from his mother: "Dear Kenny, I'm sorry you had to hear us last night but if you're going to be part of the family you'd have heard us fighting sooner or later. Love, Esther."

Part of the family? It feels too early. What has Jason told her? That is something I had not even thought about before.

When I go back downstairs, I get back into bed with Jason. As he turns over I think I hear him say: "I love you."

The next day I am back in the city. It is late at night when the phone rings.

"It's Jason," he tells me.

"Where are you?" I ask, hearing lots of people talking over jukebox music in the background.

"I have to see you," he says.

"Aren't you supposed to be at work?"

"I called in sick. I'm at a bar in the Village."

"I'll meet you at the diner," I tell him.

When we are sitting across from each other, Jason asks me: "Why didn't you respond when I told you I loved you."

"I thought you were sleeping."

"I love you," he says, looking not at me but at the table.

I am silent. Having sex with Jason is not like I remember having sex with Adam. It is not like my one night with Matthew. I am not excited with him as I was with Ya'acov. I know I didn't love Ya'acov, I could have fallen in love with Matthew, I was in love with Adam. I cannot bring myself to tell him that I love him because I do not know if what I feel is love.

"Let's go," he says.

I follow him back to where I am staying. When we get into bed he starts to kiss me and I smell the liquor still on his breath.

When our sex is over he is about to get out of bed when I pull him back by his shoulder. "I love you," I tell him.

When I say these words I think about the blurb a former teacher wrote for my first chapbook of poems: "To Kenny Fries the search for love is inextricable from the search for knowledge." Holding Jason, I have no knowledge of what I am getting myself into.

Later that week we move into my costume designer's apartment on Second Avenue, not far from the theater. She and her boyfriend are in Florida and leave us two sets of keys. We will have the place to ourselves for the rest of my stay in the city. Jason and I spend the days together, most of the time in bed with opera playing. For dinner he cooks us Indian food. At night, he goes off to work and I go see how my play is doing.

Although the month's run is well attended, no reviews appear, which is just as well since I did not like the production. The initial hope of moving it to a larger theater fizzled after the well-known actress got sick and was no longer in the cast. I have a meeting with an agent whom I invited to see the play, but nothing comes of it.

During the play's last week I bring up what has been in the back of my mind: after the run, I will be going back to San Francisco.

"I thought I'd go with you," Jason tells me.

"Go with me? What about your job?"

"That's no big deal. I can find a job out there. You sound as if you don't want me to go with you."

"No. It's not that. I'm just surprised that you want to move there with me."

By the time we leave we will have known each other three months, I tell myself. I have no idea what I'll do back in San Francisco, where nobody will have even heard about my play. I'd rather live with Jason than with the roommates I've been living with, I continue. I'd like to see if we can build a home together. The lease to the three-bedroom Victorian is mine and I just have to give my roommates notice, I decide.

"If you're serious, I'll call my roommates and tell them my new boyfriend is coming back with me and that they'll have to move out at the end of the month," I say, using the word boyfriend, meaning Jason, for the first time.

"I'm serious. I'll tell my boss tomorrow."

Jason gives two weeks' notice. He tells his parents and they ask what kind of dishes I have back in San Francisco. They offer to give us their old Melmac plates that Jason has always wanted.

When we decide he will move back West with me we go to Brooklyn to have dinner with my parents. After a vegetarian meal my mother has been kind enough to cook for Jason, we tell them about our plans. My father offers to ship Jason's things from the warehouse where he is shipping manager.

One night during the week we are to leave for San Francisco I am alone in bed. "I want to say good-bye to the guys in the bars," Jason told me earlier. "I'll see you later."

I listen to the cars pass by on Second Avenue and know that it is raining. As I drift in and out of sleep I hear the hospital elevator, familiar from long ago, open and close. I hear the nurses' footsteps on the tiled floor. I do not know what time it is when I sense Jason has come home and is beside me.

I smell the cigarettes on his skin, taste the liquor, like ether, on his tongue. I hold him as he rubs himself against me, anesthetized by long-forgotten thoughts, afraid that Jason will not come back with me to San Francisco, at the same time being afraid that he will, not knowing which causes the larger dose of fear.

I find a two-for-one Valentine's Day special fare for us to fly to San Francisco. I make arrangements to ship my car cross-country so we won't have to take the time to drive the longer southern route. It is still winter.

❧

When my father owned a women's sports clothes import company with his brothers, he went to work later than I left for school. Early in the morning, after eating breakfast, I would have a spare twenty minutes to climb onto my mother's vacant side of the bed. My father would be asleep or just waking up. Moving as close to him as I could, I used his large body to warm me.

My head underneath the cover, I heard my brother in the bathroom, and eventually my mother came into the room to tell me it was time to get dressed so I would not miss the school bus. On winter mornings, I basked in my father's warmth a few more minutes longer before I kissed him, leaped from under the covers, and sat on the edge of the bed, quickly pulling on my clothes before the warmth of my father's body disappeared.

∽

For Jason's twenty-eighth birthday, his first in San Francisco, I decide to surprise him by inviting some of my friends whom he has met to come over for some cake.

That night, when Jason comes back from a class he is taking, we all yell: "Surprise!"

Jason looks distraught and whispers for me to meet him in my bedroom at the back of the house. When I open my door he is sitting, a lost child, on my bed.

"I hate surprise parties," he tells me, looking sheepishly at the floor.

"I thought you'd feel more like it was your home if I had people over."

"I hate my birthday," he says.

"I bought a great cake," I hear myself tell him, sounding like my mother.

"I'm not going out there."

"What do you mean you're not going out there? They're here because it's your birthday."

"I don't care. I can't see anyone."

"What am I supposed to do? Tell them to leave."

"Yes."

"You're kidding." When I get no answer I know he is not kidding.

I go out to the kitchen, take a deep breath, and tell my friends that Jason does not like surprise parties and has asked me to ask them to leave. One by one, they disperse. Some linger in the hopes I will offer a piece of cake, but I don't feel right cutting it with Jason in the bedroom.

After the last person leaves I realize that Jason too has gone. Impulsively, I go outside, searching the neighborhood streets trying to find him.

When I don't see him anywhere I get into my car and drive toward the Castro Street bars, hoping I will catch Jason on his way, but again I do not find him.

Back at home, I wait until I hear his keys in the front door.

"Where were you?"

"I felt awful."

"I went looking for you everywhere."

"I called my mother."

"Your mother?"

"I didn't know who else to call. I told her what happened and she told me I should apologize."

"I'm sorry. I didn't know you had such difficulty on your birthday. Do you want some cake? It looks delicious."

"Didn't they eat it?"

"I didn't let them."

"You didn't let them?" he says as he begins to laugh. I break out in laughter, too. We eat half of the cake before we go to bed.

❧

It is the last days of LPs when I begin my opera collection. Every week, Jason and I spend entire evenings searching out the best buys at Tower Records, returning home to play different versions of the same opera. Many nights, way after midnight, we compare the dramatic renditions of Callas with the more sonorous-sounding Sutherland; we both fall for the wildly red-haired Bulgarian soprano Ljuba Welitsch, who sounds frightfully innocent and delectably mad in the final scene from *Salome*.

When we go hear Leontyne Price in recital, we sit in the third row on the aisle, and after she has sung her fifth and final encore, "Tu, tu? Piccolo iddio," the suicide aria from *Madama Butterfly*, we yell, "We love you, we love you," as she bows grandly on the stage.

On our way home from the recital Jason tries to hum the melody of an aria he wants me to know. I tell him to sing it, and slowly, shyly, and not too tunefully, he does. I have never heard him sing and he tells me he has never sung in front of anyone before.

Jason accompanies me when I'm invited to read my poetry in Los Angeles and we go to Disneyland, buying silly Mickey Mouse hats that we put on members of our growing secondhand stuffed-animal collection. Jason finds these animals on his almost daily jaunts to junk stores. He begins to buy me broken animal toys—fish without fins, windup dinosaurs that can no longer walk—which I display in a separate disabled-animal section.

On Passover we decide to make a seder, cooking for twenty-one, beginning a tradition that our friends will look forward to each year. For our first seder, Jason, still a vegetarian, cooks Indian food, forgetting to make *paneer*, the cheese needed for the main dish. The alternative Haggadah I have put together generates much discussion about liberation and multicultural traditions, and nobody notices the missing *paneer*.

But underneath all that Jason and I share grow unspoken problems, unseen currents that I cannot yet name. Three months after we move to San Francisco I get a fever. When my doctor tells me I have a sexually transmitted disease I know I caught it from Jason.

"I thought you were celibate for three months before you met me," I tell him.

"I tried," he says. "How do you know you caught it from me?"

"I haven't had sex with anyone but you since we met."

"You didn't catch it from me," he says.

It is not that I caught something from him that bothers me, but that he can't own up to the fact that I caught it from him. Mixed up with these emotions are my feelings about his having been with other men during our courtship in New York. We never talked about whether or not we would be monogamous. At the beginning of our relationship I did not want to have sex with other men. Having just got involved, why would he want to have sex with another man?

Even though I share the responsibility for the lack of discussion about monogamy, his not admitting that what he has done has caused me to be ill irks me. His having sex with other men makes me doubt his attraction to me, bringing to the surface my own unexamined feelings about my legs. The trust between us wavers, then disintegrates, as does my precarious self-esteem.

I start to swim and realize the men I meet in the showers are attracted to me. But these quick encounters leave me unfulfilled, make me realize it is Jason that I wanted, but after so many years of denial, old patterns of being too afraid to talk about what needs to be talked about add to my confusion. He no longer bathes my legs. Our sex becomes more and more infrequent. Listening to opera seems to be our only mode of communication, a replacement for the passion we once shared.

Like my family when I was growing up, if you look at our relationship from the outside there is no sign of the emotional turmoil going on. These emotions—unnamed, unexpressed, not understood—bind us tighter together. I tell myself if only I try harder I can overcome the difficulties with Jason, as I have overcome so many physical obstacles before. A dependency that neither of us acknowledge continues to grow.

What neither of us yet understands is that in a relationship without trust, love becomes distorted, no matter how strong that love may be. I have no idea how to begin the needed process of communication and understanding. Months go by without my even thinking to sit down and write. Instead I begin to physically and emotionally withdraw.

∾

After we watch *Hawaii Five-O* I follow my parents and brother into the kitchen. My mother scoops out ice cream, Sealtest vanilla, into lime green bowls with scalloped edges. My parents sit on either side of the counter between the kitchen and the dining room. My brother sits across from me at the dining-room table, the white soup tureen, never used, in the center between us.

When he gets to the bottom of his bowl, Jeffrey scrapes the dish, wanting every drop. As he scratches the spoon across the bowl's bottom, my brother begins to giggle, first uncomfortably, then continuing with menace.

"Cut it out," my mother yells from the kitchen. The sound of the metal spoon scraping the bowl is like the sound she hates most—fingernails across a blackboard—a sound that makes spines twinge.

My brother answers her with more scraping, more laughter.

In one movement my father is off his chair and whacks my brother in the head. My brother escapes around the table, the same table I am able to use to escape my father when he comes after me with his cat-o'-nine-tails, into the living room, and down the L-shaped hallway. I hear the bathroom door slam shut.

It is then I realize that my father is no longer in the room with us, but has chased my brother down the hall. My mother and I hear him trying to get to my brother behind the locked bathroom door. We hear a loud noise and a scream and I am left with my bowl of melted ice cream, alone.

"Stop it, stop it," I hear my mother screaming. "Donny, you're going to hurt him," she pleads.

Hearing a dull thud in the bathtub just behind the living-room wall, I instinctively perch myself near the telephone. I lift the receiver, but what would I say, whom would I call?

I go to the apartment door, thinking I will run to get Charlotte and Sam, or Helen, who live at the end of the hall. Then I rush back to the phone.

I do not know what I do next. I might dial 911, hanging up when the police operator answers. I might call Charlotte and Sam. Perhaps I run down the hall to get them. I see my mother ushering my brother out of the house. I see the blood coming from my brother's head. I see our neighbor Edith, her husband, Morris. I see the bathroom door, off its hinges, destroyed.

I know Morris, who doesn't drive so well, has driven my mother and brother to the emergency room at Coney Island Hospital. I wait in my bedroom for them to return.

I do not know if my father is in the house with me, or if I am alone. I know I am pacing back and forth in my bedroom, thinking a thought over and over, seeing it every which way I can turn it, trying to change it in my head. I know I pull out my bed from underneath the high-riser, preparing it for sleep. I know I hear the cars swishing by on the Belt Parkway fifteen stories below. I know that when I next see my father I say: "I hate you," words I have never used to explain a feeling I have never felt for him before.

❧

I do not know when I began hitting Jason but I am hitting him now. Perhaps that night he went cruising again in the bars and has come home long after dawn. Or he has asked to borrow money and I have declined. An argument ensues and when he gets angry he begins to yell "fidget" or "three-toed bastard," the names he knows my brother called me.

At the sound of these familiar names coming from the man with whom I have lived for almost two years, a knot of helplessness and frustration rises from my gut, and not knowing what else to do, how else to release these long-pent-up emotions, I lash out at Jason, jump on top of him, start punching him in the arm.

I know that my violence toward Jason has little to do with him, just as my brother's had little to do with me. Both can be traced to my father's violence, which in turn leads to my grandfather, whom I never knew. I know I am painfully caught at the end of at least three generations of physically abusive men and it is time for this behavior to cease.

The next day, I am back in therapy with Lu, the psychologist I stopped seeing when I went to New York for my play. "I'm here to talk about hitting my lover," I tell her.

"Did someone used to hit you?" Lu asks.

Years before, in graduate school, I told my New York psychologist that I knew I was physically abused by my brother but that I was not yet ready to deal with it. After mentioning it to her we never spoke about it again.

Now I want it to be different. Not only do I start to talk about what happened with my brother but I also talk about two close friends who are both beginning to get sick, both of whom are dying.

"How do you feel about hitting Jason?" my therapist asks.

The knot of frustration returns when I cannot find a word to answer.

"I had no way to get back at him," I tell her.

"Jason or your brother?"

"First my brother. Then Jason. Especially when he called me those names my brother used. I can't believe I trusted him."

"How does that make you feel?"

"Foolish. Angry."

"How do you feel about being hit by your brother?"

"Embarrassed," I confide. I cannot bring myself to mention my father.

∾

Without warning, a hand jostles my shoulder. Awake, I check the window to see if it is yet light. No luck. Even though the window looks out on a vacant shaft where little light ever enters, I can easily tell it is not yet dawn.

"It's time," the man who roused me tells me as he points to the wheelchair in front of him.

When I reach for my clothes his hand prevents me from getting to them. "No need," he tells me, dressing me in the discarded sheet that passes for a hospital robe.

The man wheels me into the hallway, past the nurses' station, through the locked-at-night door to the ward, and into the awaiting elevator. The hospital at night is all dim light, every sound magnified by the unfilled space of the usually too busy corridors. It is as if you are transported to the place where past, present, and future merge together so tenses do not make any sense, they do not matter. It is easy to imagine I live on a forbidden planet where nobody is able to live outside this building of many secrets and endless corridors, a planet whose inhabitants, reaching a certain age, are fated to live here in perpetuity, never growing older or younger.

The waiting room in which I am left is dark, except for a lone lit desk lamp. Also on the desk is a large open book. There is nobody present so I do not know to whom the book belongs.

When the man returns he takes a pen from his shirt pocket and crosses out what I take to be a name, my name, in the open book. He wheels me past the desk into a large room with enormous machines I have never seen before.

The man helps me get up on a long narrow table. While I am still sitting on the edge of the hard, cold table, he unties the string behind my neck and removes the flimsy sheet from my body so I am naked. He gently touches my shoulder and I realize this is his way of telling me he wants me to lie down.

The man is soon joined by another. This one carries a clipboard, which occupies his attention. The man who has wheeled me here touches the other man's shoulder as he passes him on the way to the door, which swings shut behind him.

The man with the clipboard moves behind a panel full of knobs and switches. He lifts a small lever and the table on which I am lying begins to move, ever so slowly, backward, into the tunnel in the wall behind me. As I am being moved into the wall I am the rocket ship about to be launched at the beginning of the Space Mountain indoor roller coaster at Disneyland. I am one of the deformed bodies a Nazi doctor will experiment on. I am a human time capsule being buried deep within these walls so those who come after me will know what a person with my particular disability looked like many hundreds of years from now. I am a mummy being prepared to be preserved forever.

Inside the tunnel in the wall I hear a voice speaking just above my right ear. The voice tells me to relax, hold on to the pillow if I need to. The voice disappears and the loudest noise, a combination of the rhythmic knocking of the largest rocking chair and the loudest, most abhorrent construction being done to the street directly outside your apartment window in New

York City, begins. The table slightly shakes, the tremors warning of the big earthquake that has not yet happened but you have always been expecting. I hold still, trying to discern if it is the noise that causes the shaking.

It could be the X-ray machine rolling down its metal track. The machine I am afraid will fall on top of my eight-year-old body. I feel my father's hands pressing on my legs to keep them still in the position needed for the precisely ordered X ray. When I lift my head just enough to see my father I notice he is wearing a heavy apron, not white like the one he wears when koshering a chicken in the kitchen sink, but a dark metallic gray that matches the smaller but heavy swatch that rests across my hips, guarding what resides between my legs, just above my thighs.

It is then I feel it—the sudden jolt to my arm, just below my left shoulder, and I am screaming as I recoil in horror not only from the searing of my skin—shock and fire—but terrified that it is my father who holds the metal fork, and when I am able to look at him he is a few steps away from me once again checking my mother's roast with the same fork with which he burned my arm.

∾

Even though we discover mysterious Mayan ruins and snorkel through coral reefs, swimming alongside the most colorfully phosphorescent fish, our trip to Mexico is marred by Jason's insistence on cruising for men. When I told him my plan for our three-year anniversary, we agreed that the idea was to be together, and that while in Mexico we both would refrain from having sex with other men.

After a few hours together in an empty local bar in Mérida, instead of coming back with me to the hotel, Jason goes to cruise the *zócalo*. I angrily walk the streets and encounter him with another man.

"Do you have the ticket to the bar so I can get back in?" he asks me.

"You have one yourself, don't you?"

"I need one for him," he tells me, pointing to the man at his side, who obviously does not know any English.

Not wanting to make a scene in a foreign country, I walk away.

Not even fifteen minutes later, Jason comes back to the hotel. "I guess I was pretty weird," he says.

"We agreed not to do any of this here—the trip is supposed to be for us," I remind him.

❦

Since I was tested before Jason I will be the first to know. During the past two weeks, as the day to pick up my test result has approached, I have gotten progressively sicker. This past week I've had to stay home from work with the flu. When we leave the house for the Castro, my fever still has not broken.

At the test site they will not allow Jason, even though I tell them he is my lover, to accompany me into the room in which I will find out the result. "Only the person getting the result is allowed," the counselor tells me.

I sit at the side of his desk as he moves his finger down pages of computer printout searching for the number corresponding to the number I have handed him. All that I can see are letters, mostly N, a few P, as his finger grazes page after page.

"You're negative," he tells me. "Do you want me to get your friend?"

"He's okay," the counselor tells Jason. Jason seems perplexed, surprised.

Released into the streets, I run ahead with a frightening

amount of glee. After I wait for Jason to catch up with me, I go into a corner store and buy some ice cream. We hail a taxi.

As we drive up the hill to where we have lived together for over three years, we are laughing in the backseat of the cab.

At home I call my parents, who I know have been waiting by the phone since half an hour after the time of my scheduled appointment. My mother picks up on the third ring.

"I'm negative," I shout into the phone.

"Let me get your father," she tells me. By the time he gets on the phone my mother and I, then my father, are crying, over-whelmed that, at least for now, I have remained uninfected.

The next day Jason begins to act a bit strange. When I ask him what's going on, he tells me that he is shocked that I was negative. Considering that we had unsafe sex the first few months after we met, he figured we both would have the same result. He is now, for the first time, contemplating the possi-bility that despite all his years of anonymous backroom sex in New York and Paris, he too might be negative. For this he is unprepared.

The next day I wake up with a high fever and when it is time for Jason to go get his result I am too sick to leave the house. His friend Mark goes with him and I tell Jason to call me as soon as he knows.

At the appointed time I wait by the phone. I grab it before the first ring ends.

"I'm positive."

I tell him, "Come home."

It only takes him fifteen minutes but it seems longer. Having lived all of my life with a disabled body, I have an inkling of what Jason must be feeling. I pace the room with too many thoughts, and even more questions, each leading back to another thought, and another question. Why is he positive and I negative? Neither of us—who can be?—is prepared for this. What will I say?

I meet Jason in the narrow hall, halfway between my bedroom and the front door. In silence, we hug. He seems stunned as we walk into the living room, where he sits on the couch and I sit on the floor.

He is looking down at the floor like he did the first night we met over three years ago in New York City. Then, when he first approached me in that bar, neither of us had any idea that he would be facing what he faces today.

But I wonder if unconsciously one, or both of us, knew. Who wanted to know? We didn't even know what a T cell was in 1984. But what if we did know, what then? Would I have pursued the relationship? Would Jason have moved with me to San Francisco?

"When I was born," I hear myself tell Jason, "I wasn't supposed to walk and I am able to do so now," offering him the only kind of hope that I can summon from within. I feel both our bodies tremble when I take his hand in mine.

∾

It is the summer after I graduate from college, a month before I begin graduate school, when my father's oldest brother, my uncle Al, dies after a bout with Hodgkin's disease.

When I go see my father sitting shivah, I sit across from where he sits on the traditional cardboard box. "Did you have something to eat?" he asks.

My father begins to tell me about my uncle's last night in the hospital. Sitting on the cardboard box my father begins to cry.

"Oh, Donny, don't," a woman wearing too much makeup says, putting her hand on his shoulder as she passes by on her way to get more food from the abundant platters in the kitchen.

"Let's go in there," my father tells me. He takes the box with him into the other room.

Alone with my father, I let him tell me what he needs to tell me. I sit with him and let him cry.

Then I sit next to my grandmother. "I'm so sorry, Anna," a departing woman says.

My stone-faced grandmother shakes the woman's hand, then lowers her head to my ear. "Sure, I don't see her for years but now she comes to see me in my sorrow," she tells me.

Later that summer, it is during the week when my mother is at the upstate house. I go to Brooklyn and wait for my father to come home from work. The doorbell rings.

I open the door and see a neighbor. "How is your father?" she asks me.

Confused, I tell her he's not yet back from work.

"I sat next to him on the bus this morning," the neighbor tells me.

I look at her, still having no idea what it is she is trying to tell me.

"On the bus this morning," she begins again. "Your father started to cry," she is finally able to say.

That night when my father comes home, when I tell him the neighbor came by to see how he is doing, he tells me he has been seeing a psychologist. "I've not felt well all summer, since my brother died," he confesses. "I feel dizzy. I start crying at the oddest times. I don't like being alone in the apartment all week long."

"Why doesn't Mom stay in the city with you?" I ask.

"She works hard all year and has the summer off," he says.

That summer, every Thursday my father and I meet for dinner around the corner from my apartment at the Second Avenue Deli.

From the street I see him in the small vestibule between the door and the host's table. Once inside, I nudge past those also waiting, and finally reaching him, we kiss each other hello. I notice a woman, staring.

"Are you two together?" the woman asks. "You're father and son, aren't you?" she tries again, perhaps now noticing that I look very much like my father.

"Uh-huh," we respond in unison.

"Well, I think that's just beautiful, kissing in public," the woman says. "And on the lips," she adds before going to claim her table.

❧

Each individual's experience of the body's decline is different. As our bodies begin to fail, as sooner or later all bodies do, emotions long stored beneath the skin, within our bones, are released on an often unsuspecting and uncaring world, including ourselves. Some of us rage against the inevitable loss of control, while others accept this mortal fact with a dignity that is as powerful as it is rare.

How does HIV change a life? I cut every relevant article out of the newspaper. I follow up every mention of every type of treatment, every mention of a cure. But how do I convince Jason to get a T cell count when I haven't seen an orthopedic doctor for seven years? Jason learns to cook macrobiotic, teaches me to make sweet-and-sour tempeh. We no longer share razor blades.

More. At night, sleeping next to Jason, I feel his heartbeat and imagine his blood flowing to each end of his body. I want to pour the blood from his body and cleanse this invisible thing from our lives. I want to somehow find protection. But blood takes on a whole new meaning, as does the word *positive*. When I bring up anything concerning the possibility he might get sick Jason tells me he does not want to talk about it.

I begin to think about critical mass: How much virus in the blood does it take to cause infection? Which day might be the last healthy day? We both begin to look for signs: white on the tongue, fungus between toes, a red blotch growing any-where. In the bathtub I wonder exactly how much hot water is needed to change the water from feeling cold. Outside the city I wonder precisely how much rainfall will make the stream I am watching overflow.

And more. When we argue Jason accuses me of raising his stress level, which will cause him to lose T cells. When he sweats at night we both are afraid. He gets a scare when he has trouble breathing and we spend the entire day in the emer-gency room at San Francisco General, most of the time in the waiting room, until the doctor on duty tells us Jason has bron-chitis, not pneumocystis.

Soon, he is again spending an inordinate amount of time cruising the bars, staying out late and drinking, which I recog-nize is not only his choice but his way of convincing him-self nothing much has changed. I understand his constant need to feel attractive, but his not taking care of himself, beyond the fact that this might increase his chances of getting ill, bothers me.

The damage HIV does to a body is incremental, at first unseen. Although the result is not the same, the process of the decline of my body also goes easily unnoticed. If it were possible to track these slight changes as they happen it would be like seeing time.

The body ages. Over the past few years, more and more I am walking on the side of my right foot, causing the discrepancy between my leg lengths to increase. My limp gets worse. The lunging motion when I walk begins to take its toll, mostly on my right hip and knee. Then, back problems begin.

Only pain, the body's alarm, makes me notice. My daily battle to move through the pain becomes exhausting. It seems like I am always tired. My short-term memory begins to dim. I am increasingly aware of how much I cannot control.

But early in my life, during the pain of surgery, I was

anesthetized. I didn't want to worry my parents. I learned to ignore my body's alarm. Growing up, I marched stoically through every obstacle, and twenty-eight, I am still doing so. Having Jason and his health to focus on makes my own body much easier to ignore.

His mother and sister call and ask me how he is doing. Physically he's doing fine but I'm not sure how much he wants them to know. His family is no better at communicating with each other than is mine. I know I do not want to be his family's go-between. He should be talking to them about it, not I.

When I go to a residency in Wyoming, I spend the time writing *The Healing Notebooks*, a poem sequence about our lives together since we have known that Jason is HIV-positive. After, Jason and I drive to the Southwest, hoping to get our relationship back on track.

We revisit some places that have been special to us, find some new places we enjoy. But more and more I feel that too much has transpired between us for our relationship to survive.

During the course of our almost five-year relationship, I have played the role of caretaker and parent—making sure the bills are paid on time, urging him to do what would be good for him to do. It has been a long time since we have been naked together in the bathtub. When I have needed Jason most he is usually at a sex club or a bar.

Before I go away to write again, this time for three months, we decide to use the months apart to decide whether or not we should separate or stay together. We agree not to make any decision until I return in the fall.

A month later, Jason calls to tell me that when I return to San Francisco we will have to move, our house is being sold. Soon after, I am writing the first poems directly dealing with my disability, when my lower back begins to spasm, causing a great deal of pain. I can no longer sit at a desk for long durations of time. I will no longer be able to support myself with temporary office jobs. It is time to go see a doctor to check out what is happening to my body.

The similarities between my relationship with my family and my relationship with Jason make it difficult for me to think clearly about my disability. To get a clearer picture of what I need to do to take care of myself, I need to separate from Jason, to slow down the pace of my life, to leave San Francisco and move back to the East Coast, closer to what, even after being away almost seven years, still feels like home.

Then, I am introduced to Miguel.

❧

His hand, holding mine, guides me through the crowded bar. His six-foot body navigates a narrow passage through the walls of gay men smoking, drinking, and dancing. It is Saturday night, two days after my twenty-ninth birthday.

"Don't worry about catching the last train back," he tells me. "You can spend the night at my apartment."

We find what passes for an empty place to sit against the wall. I sit and lean my back against the concrete behind me. The rest of the bar, the incessant beating of the dance rhythm, fades away and I can only hear the accent of his voice, see his face as only his shining blue eyes.

"How's your back?" he asks.

"Not so good."

"You're beautiful."

"What?"

"You're beautiful," he says again.

I shrug my shoulders, look down, not knowing what to say. I feel his hand press mine. "Let's get out of here," he says.

Back in his apartment, I am sitting in a rocking chair next to the fire. Miguel sits on the floor looking up at me. As he unlaces my shoes, removes them, I close my eyes. After he has pulled off my socks, my feet, both of them, rest naked in his open palms. I hear him put oil on his hands.

His fingers begin slowly to explore my toes. I feel his fingers slide between my toes and I am once again a small child strengthening my legs by pressing them against my father's hands.

I hear a crack. I cannot open my eyes to see what has happened to my legs because I have no eyes. I know if my hands could reach down and touch where my legs are supposed to be I would hear the crack again, if I could reach my legs I would feel them withered, twisted—the gnarled roots of an uprooted tree.

It is his kiss on the scar on my lower right leg that forces me to open my eyes. My legs glisten as they dangle in his palms. I watch him as his lips trace my scars, as his teeth delicately pull on the hair on my legs, on my thighs. He has risen up, is kneeling between my knees.

My legs embrace him, pull him closer so I can feel his smooth skin between my thighs, touch his hair as he takes me into his mouth. I rise up to go deeper and when he lifts me from the chair, my body is suspended between his body and the fire.

He carries me. We turn over, our bodies locked together, again and again, our mouths, our chests, our groins, connected in a full-bodied love I have never felt before. Never has a bed been so long, so wide.

All walls disappear and we levitate above the city. The crisp autumn air—a sudden chill. The gold leaves, and red and yellow and brown and orange float in the air with us, waiting for the fall.

The sharp pain in my back and I see him, ecstatic, as he thrusts, penetrating deeper, one more time, and I know in a few hours I will be on a plane to San Francisco, in a week he will be on his way to New York City.

Holding him, his heartbeat returning to normal, I listen but I cannot hear anything outside. Is it still night? Too early?

He is on top of me again, about to kiss me, when I stop him and hold his head in both my hands. For a short moment, the rare moment when attention is riveted in the present to what is directly before you, time is suspended, becomes all time—and then the moment has passed and his tongue is searching for mine, our bodies pressing against each other.

Then, I feel his hands once again begin to caress my legs, and find my scars.

∾

I call Jason to tell him about the physical pain I have been experiencing. I tell him I want to move back East. I ask him if he wants to move with me and he tells me because of his HIV status he thinks San Francisco is a better place for him to be. He asks me if he gets sick will I come back to take care of him.

I think about what Jason has just asked me. With my own body beginning to fail I know I will need every tangible and intangible resource I can muster to deal with whatever lies ahead.

In my mind the question shifts: If Jason got sick *could* I take care of him? Would I have the physical or emotional strength? The money? Could I even play that role well? After a long pause I tell him no.

Hanging up, I think how I have never had to say *no* like this before. I stare at the phone and think of my parents, who have always been there for me when a physical crisis has occurred. Because they never failed me should I now not fail Jason?

I feel an overwhelming guilt, compounded by my not telling Jason about Miguel, even though my decision and answer would have been the same if I hadn't met him.

I begin to mourn the loss of Jason, of what we once had—the possibility of it. I think about how I have reached the place I have reached. I think about two friends' recent deaths, about the impending loss of my San Francisco apartment, which has been safe haven, for almost seven years.

Now, as I begin to lose full use of my body, I am beginning to lose control.

ॐ

I am in session in my psychologist's office when the earthquake hits. The half minute it takes the plates beneath the earth to shift feels much longer.

"I have to take care of my body," I tell Lu.

"What about surgery?"

I am silent. I am once again that infant in the incubator. During surgery, my leg is broken. As I try to relearn to walk, I am totally dependent on others.

"What about artificial legs?" Lu asks.

"How could you say that?"

She is silent, the way psychologists can be sometimes.

"I don't think it's fair that you brought up any of this," I say. "I hoped I had left all of this behind."

More silence. "Even if that didn't mean dealing with yet more anesthesia, getting used to a different body, not to mention the scars. I haven't even come to terms with what I already have. Even then—" I stop myself midsentence.

"Even then?" she repeats.

After all I've been through, after all I've achieved, I would be admitting failure. I would no longer be who I am. I'd have to get used to a whole new identity, is what I want to say.

But the idea of different legs is too much for me to handle. I change the subject. "The only reason Jason wants me to stay is because he is afraid of getting ill," I say. "I understand his fear but I can no longer spend all my energy trying to make something unworkable turn out well. When I came back, even though I told him I was leaving, he thought we could still work things out. It's too late for that."

"Have you told him about Miguel?"

"I can't find the right time." I offer what I know is not a suitable reply. "I'm not sure I should be in this new relationship," I tell her.

"You already are," Lu tells me.

Driving home, up the familiar Seventeenth Street hill, I turn on the radio to listen to the beginning of the World Series game, which should be just about to start. Apparently, the quake was worse than I thought because the stadium is being evacuated, the game will be postponed. When I reach the top of the hill I see a fire pump spraying water with great force skyward.

When I reach my house I see a group of unfamiliar people staring at the large crack in the side of the house above the garage, examining another crack zagging through the mosaic design on the front porch between the two decorative columns. Inside there is no electricity, but not much damage.

I wonder where Jason is. He's supposed to teach tonight. Who knows when he'll be home? I expect he'll stay out prowling the Castro, drinking in the unlit bars, if they are open.

But just as it is getting dark, Jason returns. We sit on the front steps, watching unknown people pass by holding candles.

Our electricity returns at two a.m. When I wake in the morning I call the orthopedic doctor to see if she is keeping her appointments today. She is.

After examining my back and legs, after looking at the X rays, she tells me, "The right knee just isn't holding up very well. It's unstable. I'll have to consult with those more familiar with cases like yours, but at this stage I'd recommend amputation, probably both legs, from the knee down."

That night next to each other in bed, Jason says, "There's someone else, isn't there?"

I admit to him what I've wanted to tell him since returning to San Francisco over two weeks ago. I assure him that I made the decision to separate before I met Miguel. Jason quietly gathers his pillows and blanket and moves into the other room. Left alone in bed I wonder if he will ever talk to me again.

Months later, Jason will tell me how afraid he was because being HIV-positive he would never meet another man. If I knew this would I have gone ahead with leaving? He will tell me that even at the end he was still attracted to me, that he still loved me. Months later, it will still be difficult for me to tell the difference between love and the fear of being alone.

But that sleepless night, even though I realize Jason has replayed his relationship with Eddie all over again, I feel that in my first adult love relationship I have been a miserable failure. Like Shabtai in Israel when he left his wife and daughter, I realize that by taking care of yourself, you might at the same time hurt others.

Years later, after telling my parents all the painful truths I have come to learn, this fact haunts me even more. But now I know I can no longer afford to deny what my body wants me to know.

∾

Back East, I make an appointment to see Dr. Frankel, who has become chief of orthopedics at the Hospital for Joint Diseases.

Dr. Frankel confirms the fact that the lumbars in my lower back have degenerated because of the length discrepancy between my legs. He tells me that although I now walk on the side of my right foot, and the angle from which it juts out from my leg has increased to almost ninety degrees, my knees are holding up very well.

"Am I causing any harm to my body?" I ask him, trying to allay one of my fears.

"Nothing irreparable," is his reply.

Dr. Frankel tells me there is now a way not only to safely rotate my right foot underneath my leg to be in normal weight-bearing position, but to lengthen both legs, and to erase the imbalance between them, as well. To do so he will use the Ilizarov method, a surgical procedure of orthopedic reconstruction for which he has become well known.

He gives me a brochure that describes the procedure begun by Russian surgeon Gavriel A. Ilizarov, in order to save limbs of veterans after World War II. Dr. Frankel has become the first orthopedic surgeon in the United States to perform this procedure on an adult patient. The procedure consists of cutting the shell, the cortex, of the bone, but leaving the bone's marrow cavity, which contains important blood vessels necessary to the formation of new bone, intact.

During surgery, the Ilizarov apparatus, consisting of wires, is put through the bone, and external rings, which are kept under a great deal of tension, are used so that the rings better support the bone. With the slow traction applied by the apparatus, the nerves, muscles, and tendons, as well as the bone, grow.

"Basically, what you do when you use the Ilizarov method," Dr. Frankel says, "is turn back the clock to fetal days. You have an almost fetal-like growth of new and viable tissues.

"The apparatus itself must be devised before surgery in order to see exactly how it should look and how it will fit. When you have to work with a complex deformity, you have to do a great deal of precise and careful preplanning. There is a great deal of precision to the apparatus. The patient must be able to move the limb that is supported by the apparatus and be able to bend and twist."

I slowly realize the import of what I am being told. By osteogenesis, new bone growth, occurring spontaneously and bridging the space forced open by the Ilizarov apparatus, surgery can now bypass the problem that Dr. Milgram faced in rotating my right foot to normal weight-bearing position. Dr. Milgram's concern about having to cut out a portion of my bone so he could rotate my foot, thereby losing even more length in my right leg and increasing the discrepancy between my legs, led him to postpone the operation year after year. Now, through use of the Ilizarov method, Dr. Milgram's long-held fear can, at least theoretically, be allayed.

In describing the procedure to me, Dr. Frankel also tells me that a good deal of cooperation from the patient is needed. "The patient must exercise, a lot of weight-bearing exercise must be performed," he says, "because such exercise promotes new bone growth."

When I ask him about complications he informs me there is some risk of infection and sometimes a great amount of pain, though he is quick to highlight the section of the brochure that quotes his first patient, Cheryl T. When asked about pain Cheryl T. replied, "Enough," not excruciating or extremely painful, the brochure proudly says.

"Patients do require pain medication for a number of weeks until they get on their feet," the brochure goes on to say. "You have to be ready for this," Dr. Frankel adds.

"Can I do this at any time?" I ask.

"As long as I'm around to do the job," my doctor, approaching sixty, tells me.

My temperature begins to rise just contemplating the operation. "I'll have to think about it," I tell him.

The brochure in my sweaty hand, I leave the hospital. In the backseat of a taxi, I think what it would be like to enter a hospital for surgery again, to again be anesthetized, put my body through yet another invasive procedure when I have not yet come to terms with what, years ago, already transpired. I try but cannot imagine my legs with a new constellation of individuating scars.

"Let me out here," I abruptly tell the taxi driver a bit too loudly. We just passed a hospital supplies store on Second Avenue and I remember Dr. Frankel told me a cane may help me get around until I can decide.

After being apart for three months, Miguel and I move to Provincetown at the end of Cape Cod.

That first night I am in bed, on my stomach reading a book, when I feel him press up against me. Before I know what he is doing he is inside me. With my right hand dangling off the bed I search the floor for the empty condom wrapper, but swinging my arm back and forth all I can feel is the brittle indoor-outdoor carpet.

"It feels so good," he tells me and, unprotected, I let him continue until he is going to come. I tell him to pull out.

"I want to do it all the way inside you," he tells me.

"I'm not sure we should do that again," I tell him, feeling uncomfortable with the risk I have just taken.

I am taking risks with Miguel that surprise me. Risks I have not taken since the onset of AIDS. I know that Miguel's being negative—can I trust him?—is not the sole reason. With him, as at the beginning of my relationship with Jason, I am easily enticed by the passion, the sex, as well as the danger.

Now, this is compounded not only by the awe in which I hold my new lover's beauty, but by my still unresolved feelings about my body, now boiling closer to the surface, where they threaten to overflow if I do not give in to the attention they demand. Having good sex with Miguel is quickly becoming a new way to quiet the noise, the unnamed currents of self-hatred and anger with which I regard my body.

When I return from the osteopath I can barely get down the three steps to our house. Building up my right shoe so that when I walk my two legs are the same length has caused problems in my neck and spine. Today's visit was for my second adjustment, the osteopath's attempt to manipulate my body, to raise my right hip to the same level as my left, so that my back will not be as wrenched, become unaligned, when I walk. This might help alleviate the pain.

As the afternoon progresses my body grows continually stiffer until by early evening I can barely move, a tin man in desperate need of oil.

I make my way, slowly, into the living room and begin to watch *Die Walküre*, the second installment of the Metropolitan Opera's Ring cycle being broadcast on four successive nights on public television this week. I take a cushion from the sofa and lie prone on the floor, figuring this will be the best position for my quickly stiffening body to recline.

Sometime near the end of the second act I realize my body cannot move, has become like stone. Stuck on the floor I search for the phone and realize I am too far away to get to it and I will not be able to make a call. I try to attend to the singing on the screen, and even though I already know the opera's outcome, I am caught up wondering if Brunnhilde, against her father's wishes, will intervene and defend Sieg-mund's incestuous love affair with Sieglinde.

Of course Brunnhilde does intervene, and in the next act by the time Wotan begins to sing his almost half-hour-long farewell, encircling his beloved daughter with fire, I have to pee very badly. But there is no way I can get up off the floor, no way I can make my way into the bathroom only a short distance behind me.

When Wotan relents, gives in to his daughter's plea by allowing a hero someday to retrieve her from the fire—and I know it is this hero with whom she will eventually fall in love, an entire five-hour opera later, I could tell her—it is already close to midnight, and the pain in my bladder is like when I had a kidney stone.

Thankfully, when the opera ends, Brunnhilde having been put to sleep and surrounded by flames, the extra minutes before midnight are used to replay a Jessye Norman concert performance of "The Liebestod," the love-death finale from *Tristan und Isolde.* The slow build of the aria, suspended chord to suspended chord, conducted ever so slowly, mirrors the incessant, increasing pressure of my bladder, the sharp pain having moved downward into my groin.

I attempt to roll over, thinking that the momentum will, perhaps, leave me close enough to the bathroom door. When this attempt to change my position fails I realize that the toilet is at the far end of the bathroom, anyway, and even if I could get to the bathroom door it would do me little good.

The public television station has signed off for the night and the steadily blaring buzz, which seems to get louder the longer you listen to it, begins its nightly hum. A band of primary colors above a band of stark black has replaced Jessye Norman's love-death on the screen. The noise seems to reach deafening proportions.

Two hours later Miguel opens the front door.

"What the hell is going on?" he says. "It sounds like the smoke alarm went off. What are you doing on the floor?"

"I have to go to the bathroom," I tell him.

"So, why . . . ?" He trails off, no longer needing an answer.

"Give me your hand," he says, bending down to reach for me.

I extend both arms upward, at right angles to the rest of my horizontal body, and as if we are long-familiar dance partners, Miguel easily lifts me from the floor. As he carries me in his arms I want to kiss him but the smell of alcohol on his breath is not enticing.

"Call me when you're finished," he tells me after standing me close to the toilet. As I pee it feels as if I am having an orgasm, one of those painful ones that make you think you have syphilis or gonorrhea. I hear Miguel go outside to smoke a cigarette.

When I'm finished and Miguel has retrieved me from the bathroom, he carries me upstairs and places me in our bed.

"Don't do that again," he warns me.

As I fall asleep I make a mental note to buy a portable phone.

❧

It is April when the movie theater first opens for the season. Just this past week, after two months of my supporting him on the little I have, Miguel found a job, and we decided to sign a year's lease on our rustic two-story A-frame.

When the movie is over I feel a sadness that I know is not related solely to what I have watched for two hours on the screen. When the credits have finished rolling I do not get up. I feel as if my body is dead weight. I do not have the strength to lift my body out of the chair.

Finally, I stand up, retrieve my cane from the side of the seat, and make my way to the back of the auditorium. When I go into the bathroom the lobby is already empty; the lone lights reflect off the turned-off popcorn machine.

As soon as I lock the latch on the bathroom-stall door and look at the white porcelain toilet, all that has happened since I decided to leave San Francisco begins to replay itself inside me. I am once again in bed with Jason, who is asking me if I am involved with another man. The guilt commingles with the thrill of having sex with Miguel. As I stare into the toilet I cannot peel the layers of memory, each sudden infusion of feeling after feeling, from each other.

I know that my body is trying to tell me something—letting me know that all that has happened that I have not yet dealt with, every unanswered question, along with what has been kept hidden beneath my cavalier veneer, all that has not yet been named, is beginning, all at the same time, to demand attention in the clear light of day.

A sharp twinge in my lower back reminds me where I am. Since seeing Dr. Frankel the pain in my lower back has been getting worse and worse, causing more short-term memory loss—I can't remember my own phone number. Whereas before I was able to live totally on my own, independent of anyone's assistance, I am now increasingly becoming dependent on others, especially Miguel, to do routine daily tasks I used to take for granted. The thought of surgery once again enters my mind.

I know the movie theater is about to close but I cannot move. I imagine the Ilizarov apparatus fastened through skin and bone around my leg—why don't I remember wearing braces?—and I begin to laugh, whether out loud or to myself I am not sure, and then everyone on the street outside is laughing, all the young children I have met on so many streets all during my life, the ones who point and stare, the ones who ask their mothers questions about why the man is so short, why does the man have legs like that, why are his shoes so funny, the ones who running toward me stop in their tracks when they see my deformed body, the ones who run quickly back to their fathers for protection because the sight of my body scares them.

When I begin to sweat, have difficulty breathing, I muster up one burst of energy and with what seems one concentrated motion am able to escape from the stall, from the bathroom, from the movie theater, and propelled by some unconscious force within me I am able to reach my car.

Inside the car I look back at the deserted street. I look to the harbor and open the window to hear the waves, one after another, slap against the shore.

I came to Provincetown hoping to get away from the noise caused by what other people think about my body, to finally feel what it is *I* feel. But there is no longer any protection from what I feel, what others feel, or what I imagine them to feel.

Like someone with a failing immune system, all boundaries between myself and the world are disintegrating. Undifferentiated, everything everyone has ever felt and everything I imagine them to feel, the pain my body experiences today, and the pain I experienced long ago, enter me all at once as sharply as my lovers' fingers, as confidently as the surgeons' hands. My body can no longer encompass them all.

❧

We are in New York because I am reading to celebrate the publication of *The Healing Notebooks*. Two nights before the reading, I go out with Adam; Miguel eats dinner with some of his friends. We agree to meet at eleven at a café in the Village.

Adam hangs out with me until eleven-thirty. Miguel has still not arrived. When the café closes at midnight and there is still no sign of him, Adam walks me to where I am staying.

When we reach the building, I ask Adam to stay with me awhile.

After two, I hear a knock on the door. It is an obviously very drunk Miguel. "What's he doing here?" he asks brusquely.

"I think you'd better go," I tell Adam, not wanting him to see what I know is going to be an ugly scene.

"Will you be okay?" Adam asks. I nod to assure him, give him a hug. "Call me," he says as I close the door.

"So, you two are fucking around," Miguel says, displacing his behavior with that of my own. He takes off his clothes, revealing his smooth pink skin.

"That's absurd. He's one of my oldest friends." I follow him into the bedroom.

"You were supposed to meet me at eleven."

"Big deal. I see you kept yourself occupied."

There is no use continuing to have a conversation with him when he is drunk. I go into the bathroom, hoping by the time I come out he will have fallen asleep.

Revelation can happen in the strangest places. I am sitting on the toilet in a friend's apartment on West Twelfth Street in New York City when it hits me: you do not know you are in denial until it has ended. Miguel is an alcoholic. I have been charmed by him, seduced by his acceptance of my legs, silenced by his exquisite body. My vanity, wanting to be involved with this beautiful and passionate Spanish artist, has led me astray. I am caught in a situation I still know very little about, a relationship I know is bound to disintegrate. For this I left San Francisco, I think as I examine the absurd possibility that what is happening is punishment for leaving Jason. Have I once again mistaken love for the fear of being alone?

I get up to put my cold hands above the radiator, needing to warm my body, which has begun to shiver. The steam heat, hissing as it uncontrollably escapes the pipes, barely does the job.

In the bedroom Miguel is asleep beneath the covers. I take off my clothes and join him in the bed. His body provides the warmth I need, but I cannot sleep. The familiar smell of liquor is released with his every breath. I imagine the man—or men— he probably had sex with earlier in the night. I know they all have perfect bodies.

When he wakes up in the morning he pulls me over to him and places my hand on his erection. When we have sex everything feels as if it will be all right again.

I do not yet know how long it takes action to catch up to awareness. But later that day, when neither of us speaks a word about what happened last night, even though I do not know how long it is going to take, I know this is the beginning of the end.

❧

It is after three o'clock in the morning and Miguel is still not home. Usually, when he goes out to drink after work, he returns shortly after one, when the bars close. I listen for his approaching van, the van he bought when he was awarded the grant I wrote for him only two months ago.

After four o'clock I begin to imagine he is lying drunk on the front steps of a Commercial Street store that closed hours before. It is after five when I begin to imagine what the man he is fucking looks like. After six I hear his van.

Then he is trying to open the door. Of all the sounds I've learned to identify, I know none better than the sound of someone drunk trying to unlock a door. When he finally manages to get inside I hear the faucet running.

He comes upstairs, along with the smell of cigarettes and liquor.

"Where have you been?" I ask from my side of the bed.

"It's too late for your Lucia di Lamermoor routine," he says.

"Where were you?" I ask, trying again.

"I went to a party and fell asleep on someone's couch."

I immediately know that is a lie.

"I know you've been with someone."

He does not respond.

"Who is he?" I ask, beginning to put the quick phone calls, the odd messages, together.

"A Dutch tourist. I'll never see him again."

I get out of bed and get dressed. As I make my way down the steps, I know I can no longer live in this house. The steps are too much for me to manage on my own. Dr. Frankel told me to limit stairs. What made me think I could live here?

I drive to the ocean. Watching the unceasing waves during what must be high tide, I know that I must make the decision to leave Miguel separate from whether or not I feel physically able to live on my own. Watching the seagulls skim the surface of the water searching for their morning food, I know I must move out. The rest will somehow have to take care of itself. Determined, I drive back home.

When Miguel gets up I am waiting for him in the kitchen. "Do you think you have a problem with alcohol?" I ask him.

"I don't drink too much," he tells me. "I'm European."

"Are you willing to see a therapist with me?"

"Are you kidding?"

"I'm moving out."

"Why are you doing that?"

"I need to find a place of my own."

"Don't make such a big deal about what happened last night."

"It's more than last night," I tell him. "I can't handle your drinking and since you don't think it's a problem—"

He slams his hand on the table, causing a plate to fall and break on the floor. Knowing the situation could turn dangerous, I go outside.

That day I begin my search for a new place to live, seeing dead end after dead end. Finding an accessible apartment, a place in which I can physically manage, especially in a town as old as Provincetown, is not easy.

After I see yet another place that will not suffice, I return home and Miguel asks me, warily, how my search is going.

"Not very well," I tell him, not wanting to say more. That week, this scene repeats dozens of times, during which once or twice I let the tears of frustration and fear escape from my eyes.

By the end of the week, after seeing far too many apartments, through an acquaintance of an acquaintance I find a ground-floor apartment that, living on Social Security, I can barely afford.

When I tell Miguel I've found a place, he sits next to me on the couch and kisses my hand. "Are you sure this is what you want to do?"

Looking at his large blue eyes, I am tempted, yet again, to ignore what I know to be the right move, to give in to my desire.

"I don't want to but I have to," I tell him, looking away.

"You amaze me," he says. "Time after time you come home so disappointed. I'd watch you get upset, then pick yourself up and go back out there to look at yet another apartment."

He has never said anything like this to me before. His acknowledgment of what I have been dealing with the past week removes some of the tension stored in my body. I rest my head on his shoulder and he begins to play with my hair.

ᴖ

The night before I am supposed to move, I wake up in the middle of the night with a fever close to 104. It is like when I was an infant, getting a fever the night before surgery, I tell my parents, who came up earlier that day to help me.

The next day, the friends I have lined up to help with their truck begin to load my boxes. After they bring my stuff to my new apartment they come back for more. Having no large pieces of furniture to move, by three o'clock all my belongings are in the living room of my new one-bedroom furnished apartment down an alley off Commercial Street.

My fever has come down to 101. But even without a fever I would be physically unable to help my parents unpack my suitcases and boxes.

Resting on the couch, I hear my father putting things away in the kitchen, my mother doing the same in the bedroom. Up since four, exhausted by what the doctor this morning told me was a bad case of the flu, I fall asleep.

When I get up I am not sure how much time has passed. It

seems that most of the unpacking has been done. I get up and go into the bedroom. I peer into the closet, open up some drawers.

"I can't bend down to the bottom drawer," I tell my mother.

"Where else am I supposed to put it?" she responds.

"You know Dr. Frankel said I'm not supposed to bend."

I go into the kitchen and, as I expected, my father has put things up in the cupboards, out of my reach. But knowing I could not do this on my own and thankful for what my parents have done, I quell my anger and frustration that my parents still cannot understand the physical limitations of their disabled son.

∾

I know it is time when, even if I can get out of bed by late afternoon, I cannot get myself out of my bedroom. It has been almost three weeks since my parents helped me move in. Because I can dress and bathe myself I have been turned down by the personal-assistance program that I had been counting on to shop, clean the house, help me do the things I need to do.

Because of the pain in my lower back I cannot lift anything. I can barely bend. Even though I have not eaten for what seems like days I know there is garbage rotting, waiting to be taken outside. For days I have not even opened the blinds.

Outside I imagine the scene to be like a Fellini movie. Everyone in town is peering through my windows, pointing at me. From the main street, a hundred yards away, everyone I know, and some who do not know me, have gathered to stare at me inside my house, waving their fingers back and forth, chiding me, as pathetic carnival music grinds ever so slowly. I am the freak in the center of all three rings, as well as the star of the sideshow, in a traveling circus that should have closed down a very long time ago.

I reach for the phone and Adam answers. "I'll be on the next bus up," his voice tells me.

I notice the red light on my answering machine going on and off, on and off, as if frantic to draw my attention. I know what the machine is trying to tell me. I know today is when Miguel moves in with the Dutch boy. Not knowing what else to do I begin to masturbate thinking about Miguel fucking the Dutch boy.

I do not know what the Dutch boy looks like, only once heard a message he left for Miguel on our machine. I imagine him very tall, very thin, very blond. I try to remember Miguel's face.

I hear banging on my door, but I cannot answer it. Someone calls my name. Louder. His voice tells me he knows I am inside.

The rest of the day blurs by. Perhaps I have spoken with my mother on the phone. Or the doctor. I know I have taken my pills, one every three hours, and since I spoke to Adam I have taken two, so I know his bus will be here soon.

∾

It is two a.m. and I am up in bed, waiting. The clock tells me it has been fifteen minutes since I woke up plagued, yet again, by the scene in which I am passed from hand to hand, all attention on my deformed legs. Outside my apartment, the horrible carnival music still plays much too slowly, much too loudly, a laugh box gone awry. When I become accustomed to my rapid heartbeat, I sit up in bed and realize Adam has not yet returned.

Adam arrived two days ago and the day after tomorrow I will, finally, check myself into the psych ward. Since his arrival, I have spent hours on the phone with various doctors and administrators at various hospitals.

Tonight Adam needed a break from caretaking and went out. I remember those nights of waiting for Jason, wondering if every noise was his return, or just the last streetcar of the

N-Judah line passing half a block away before heading into the tunnel on its way downtown.

I am in San Francisco, in our three-bedroom Victorian apartment on Carl Street, four blocks from Haight, in my bedroom overlooking the backyard with the lone short-stumped palm tree, when sometime around four a.m. I hear Jason fumbling with his keys down the long hallway. My closed door will let him know that I do not want to sleep with him and he should spend the rest of the night in the small bedroom halfway down the hall.

When I hear him in the kitchen I get up and go to the bathroom, even though I do not have to go. I know that Jason spends his nights in sex clubs, has sex with other men, including one who lives on our street just a few doors away. Tonight, I want to know how drunk he is.

In the hallway, as I go into the bathroom, I smell the cigarette smoke deposited on Jason's clothes at the bars and I am outside the dilapidated A-frame, bedroom upstairs, bathroom down, where Miguel goes to smoke, where we lived together less than a month ago, here in Provincetown. It is the night when Miguel has not come home at two, or three, or four, the night he first fucks the Dutch boy.

This night becomes every night, all the nights staring at the broken arm of the woman adorning the lamp on my mother's side of the bed—the glue would not hold—listening for the elevator beyond the metal door to open then close, my parents' footsteps in the echo chamber of the hall, and all the nights waiting before surgery, the incessant rhythmic squeaking of the nurses' rubber-soled shoes on hard tile, the muffled voices of the night-shift workers standing underneath the lone fluorescent light fixture, buzzing, the ecstatic moans of all the men I have known in the passionate moments they have shared with other men, the screams from patients who can tolerate their bodies racked with pain, those who can wait no longer.

∾

The purpose of my being in the hospital is to slow things down. I need a silence quiet enough, deep enough, so I can begin to hear what it is *I* think, to know what it is *I* feel, to gain some control over what has been going on.

"I hear you're a writer," a nurse tells me one afternoon.

I do not know how to respond. I do not want to respond. What the nurse has casually said has angered me.

"I don't want to talk about that," I finally say a bit too harshly. She will repeat my response to the rest of the staff at their weekly meeting. How will I explain my response to my psychiatrist when she confronts me? How can I describe my wanting to be only my body—to have no identity, no label, pinned on me? I need to shed any shred of external clue so I can discover, as if for the first time, who actually I am.

In group therapy that afternoon I am practicing keeping quiet. As the other patients talk I squash all the things my mind tells me to say. When Margo, the African-American law student who looks like a fashion model, talks about her not liking herself, I want to scream at her, shake some sense into her so she will know how beautiful and smart she obviously is.

The group leader is trying to convince the elderly Jewish woman, Ruth, who nightly roams the halls with another elderly Jewish woman, Claire, to take the shock treatments the doctor recommends to help lift her depression. Ruth tells him how worthless she is. She tells him how she has not visited her son's grave since he was killed in an auto accident over thirty years ago. Since the police told her the news, not once has she been able to cry.

"Look at him," Ruth is saying, and I realize she is pointing at me. "He has something to live for," she tells the group leader.

"He's young, he's handsome, what is he doing here with us, anyway?"

What are any of us doing here? I wonder, but my thoughts are too unfocused, I am too exhausted to provide myself with a suitable answer.

"What would you like to know from the group before we end today?" the group leader is asking me.

I want to tell Margo how beautiful she is. I want to tell Ruth she should meet my paternal grandmother, that instead of shock treatments she should go visit her son's grave. I want to tell Philip that when I met him I wanted to have sex with him but that passed and I'm glad that he is the other gay man on the ward. I want to tell Tom, who has shared my room with me the past week, how I enjoy doing the Sunday *New York Times* crossword puzzle together, how his easy acceptance of sharing such close quarters with me has helped in my quest to accept myself. I want them to know how I am beginning to see aspects of myself in all the other patients on the ward. I want to tell them how afraid I am. But all I can manage to ask is: "Have I said too much today?"

❧

"I don't remember when it stopped," I tell Dr. Riskin when she asks me when my father stopped being violent. "One day he changed. He still got angry."

"How old were you?" she asks.

"About fourteen, fifteen, maybe," I offer.

"Was that when your brother left the house?"

I make the age calculations in my head and realize that yes that must be when my brother left to go to school.

"That often happens," Dr. Riskin tells me. "One of the children leaving the house breaks the pattern."

"It's as if that part of my father disappeared."

179

❧

"First, you'll feel good for one minute a day," the nurse tells me during my last days in the hospital, "then the next day, you'll feel good for a minute and a half."

In bed the night before I am to go home I think about the group therapy session that afternoon, how the other two patients who are going home will be picked up by a husband or a parent. When I leave the hospital tomorrow it will be the first time I leave a hospital alone. It will be the first time no one is expecting me. There is no one who waits for me at home.

I drive back to Provincetown and finish the intake interview with the nurse sent from the state rehabilitation office, the first thing on my schedule for my first day at home. My social worker has made sure that when I leave the hospital I will finally have the help I need with tasks my body no longer allows me to accomplish alone: cleaning the house, food shopping, the laundry.

My first days out of the psych ward move ever so slowly. The day-by-day recovery from depression is not like a film run in slow motion but is as if the experience of every movement, every observation, is magnified. Every small, simple task completed, whether getting out of bed or walking from room to room, takes on an importance greater than the task demands.

Like the process of how skin heals from a painful blister, most of this healing is unseen, happens from within. Only when my daily life has already returned to something more familiar do I notice the depression has lifted. I look carefully at the patterns of my days to discern the new layer that underneath has grown, replacing the wounded older skin.

To this day it still takes me an inordinate amount of time to enter a swimming pool. I still cannot simply jump and in one motion begin to swim. Instead, I start out at the shallow end, first dipping in a toe, then another. Very slowly, body part by body part, I enter the water, occasionally reaching down and cupping water in my hands and pouring it over the part of my body that has not yet been wet.

Before I checked myself into the hospital I did not want to eat. I could not sleep. Now, back home, I build my days around sleeping, sometimes late into the afternoon, and by eating when the nausea subsides, usually by three p.m. The days when I cannot keep down a meal I add an envelope of instant breakfast to a tall glass of milk, or fill my stomach with saltines, to feel that I have been able to nourish my body at least that much that day.

These days there are no blurred edges. The world is in sharp focus, almost harshly so. My vision, though not wide, is clear. Colors are luminous, textures acute. I arrange my days around daily tasks: my pills, the *New York Times*. Observations: the dazzling sun on the rich blue harbor. Appointments: my psychologist, the housekeeper who cleans my house and helps me shop for food. I look forward to my parents' nightly call.

During the night, panic attacks keep happening but they no longer cause me to be afraid. I know my heart racing is just that, nothing more. No heart attack or stroke is going to occur. I try not to force my body to do anything it is not ready to do.

Then the cravings begin. After seeing my psychologist I am not only hungry but I am hungry for spare ribs. I drive to the Chinese resaurant nearby and eat an order of spare ribs, dipping each one, as well as some crispy noodles, in duck sauce. Then I am hungry for doughnuts, and on my drive home I search out Hostess white powdered doughnuts, the only doughnuts that will satisfy my particular longing.

I screen all my phone calls and only talk to those friends whom I have already told what I have been through, writing letters to some who do not yet know. I begin to see my friends.

Not in groups, where I become overwhelmed when my attention is divided, but for short visits, one friend at a time.

Time begins, first slowly, then faster, to speed up again. With the help of my state-supported housekeeper, I learn to manage with my physical limitations, get accustomed to living alone.

FOUR

A Difference in Time

One with a scar, do not think him healed.

—SWAHILI PROVERB

$\mathcal{J}$ AM alone when the hurricane begins. Earlier, I heard about the hurricane's approach on the radio while driving into town. When I stopped off to mail a letter I was confronted by the sign on the counter: POST OFFICE WILL CLOSE AT NOON TO PREPARE FOR HURRICANE'S ARRIVAL. That's when I started to take the hurricane seriously.

I return home just before noon and turn on the television. I watch the weather channel as the weatherman charts the hurricane's course.

Close to one p.m., the cable television loses reception. The electricity soon follows. At the window I stare out at the wind, which is beginning to howl a crescendo. There is not much rain. There won't be much rain, the weatherman informed us. The rain will be to the west, on the other side of the hurricane's curve.

At the window, I watch a neighbor dodge the steady gusts of wind as he crosses over the gravel alley. Peeking out the front door, I make sure my car has not yet turned over. It is still upright, solidly standing idle in the storm.

I return to the window and am once again transfixed by the wind made visible by the shaking of the large pine tree it begins to uproot. Everything outside seems horizontal. Green dirt splatters on the window. Sidling down the pane it looks like pesto. The house begins to shake and, even though this is not a tornado, I cannot help thinking about Dorothy in Kansas.

I go into my bedroom, get under the covers, listen to the climaxing wind, the walls rattle. I spend hours in bed, like so many hours since returning from the hospital. I have learned how to wait for the storm to end.

Three hours later it is over. Or because the house no longer rattles I think it is. The house seems still. I do not hear any wind.

Emboldened by the sudden silence, I get up slowly, make sure my feet are stable before walking to the window. Outside all is silent. Through the impestoed window I see, past some felled trees, a few yellow-slickered figures on the street.

As I open my front door I expect the world to change to color, just like it does for Dorothy when she lands in Oz. Not noticing any such changes, I venture forth from the door, touch my still upright car, which looks like it has been unearthed after years of being buried, and slowly walk to the street at the end of the gravel drive.

I notice the now exposed roots of the tree outside my house, the one I stared at as it shook in the wind. I notice that it tilts ominously toward the large red house in which I live. I see up close other trees, debranched, lying on the ground. Reaching the street, I see that one tree's roots have broken through the concrete sidewalk that once surrounded it. This tree now leans against the destroyed second-story porch of the house in front of mine.

As I look down the street I see a woman get out of a car. "Come out, come out, wherever you are?" I cannot keep the *Wizard of Oz* dialogue from playing in my mind. "And see the young lady who fell from a star." I look around, expecting to see munchkins, if not the bubble that carries Glinda, the Good Witch of the North, to and fro.

"Must be the eye of the storm," the woman says.

"Did you stay in there?" I ask, pointing to her car.

"I was driving to meet my friends when it started. I figured I better stay put. Luckily there was a parking place," she tells me.

"Are you all right?"

"I think so."

"I wonder if it's safe to stay outside?"

"My friends are probably wondering where I am."

"You can use my phone if it works," I tell her.

As we turn to walk toward my house, I see a few people running down the street.

"What's going on?" I call to a man as he passes by.

He turns around and, jogging backward, tells us there's a lot of damage on the east end of town. "The roof came off the motel and is floating in the swimming pool," he calls before he is too far away for us to hear him.

As I turn back to the woman who emerged from the car I notice her license plate is from Kansas. When she is finished making her call I manage to restrain myself from asking her name.

ॐ

I reach my parents' house in the Catskills the night before Thanksgiving. This is the first Thanksgiving I will spend with my family since I was in college ten years ago.

I cannot remember the last time I saw Jeffrey. He is expected later tonight. The house is small, two bedrooms and a bathroom off a living room and kitchen. When I told my parents I wanted to be with them for Thanksgiving they decided to give me their room, where I would feel safe. They will sleep on the pullout sofa in the living room.

It is late and I am in my parents' bed reading when I hear my brother's voice. It would be best to get it over with tonight but I decide to make believe I am asleep and turn out the lights.

In the morning I hear everyone awake when I get up. I put on my robe and get up to make sure both doors to the room are locked and get back into bed. When I hear my brother's voice I cannot move. I feel my heartbeat quicken, my temperature begin to rise. I reach for my pills on the night table, place two of them under my tongue. Waiting for them to take effect, I call Adam.

"Where are you?" he asks.

"Upstate. In my parents' bed. I've locked the doors. He's outside."

Adam and I begin to laugh realizing how preposterous this is. "Okay. He's here, I'm here, and what's happened in the past has already happened and isn't happening now, right?" I say when our laughter subsides.

"It's great that you're doing this," Adam reminds me.

"I wish I felt that way."

In the adjoining bathroom, I take a shower and get dressed; then I come back into my parents' room. I look at myself in the mirror and run my hand through my hair, making sure I look okay.

I close my eyes, take a deep breath, and try to imagine what will happen—how will I react?—when I see my brother.

When I realize I cannot predict what will happen, I finally open the door.

ॐ

At the table my brother and father are finishing breakfast; my mother is busy in the kitchen. It is Thanksgiving morning and I cannot remember the last time my family has gathered together in the same room. My head down, I count the fake parquet tiles of the dark brown carpet as I approach the table.

"I brought something for you to see," are Jeffrey's first words before getting up to retrieve what he is talking about.

As I sit at the table I think about the toy my brother once bought for me at Tony's, the corner store near the junior high school we both attended. I cannot remember what the toy was, but I still see myself, under my brother's watchful eye, opening it on the emerald green astroturf-like living-room carpet in the Cropsey Avenue apartment in Brooklyn.

If I can just remember the toy, visualize it, perhaps I can let go of all that has happened between us, move the relationship from the past tense into the present. If I had one good thing that I could hold on to, would I be able to accept and forgive?

"There's juice," my mother calls. I go to the kitchen and get the small glass of orange juice, drink it down before returning to the table. Jeffrey has come back holding a book, which he places in front of me.

I read the book's title: _Salaries of College Professors._

"It's a survey done last year," my brother tells me. "I thought you'd be interested in it. Look up Brandeis," he says. I have little interest in the book but open it and do as my brother has suggested. As I stare at the average salary of the average Brandeis professor I cannot see the figures on the page.

"They get paid well," I hear my brother say.

Why am I looking at this book?

"Check out the school I teach at." My brother is now directing me to the page that lists the Pennsylvania school where he teaches. He stands behind me turning the pages. I keep my head down, continue to stare at the pages as they go by.

"Move it out of the way," my mother says as she brings a bagel, with lox and cream cheese on it, to the table before going into the bathroom.

When was the last time I saw my brother—my dorm in college, his dorm at his college? I hear my mother running water in the shower as I sense the edge of my memory begin to stir.

"I've got to check the new furnace," my father announces.

When I realize I am going to be left alone with my brother I feel my heart try to beat faster, but the two pills in my system rein it in, take control. I hear the porch door close.

I am still sitting at the table with my brother's book in front of me. Where is Jeffrey?

"Did they tell you I was in the hospital?" I hear myself say.

"You're not disabled," my brother says from somewhere on the other side of the room. "I watched one of those shows on TV and you're not like them, you're too smart. I even saw your Dr. Frankel on one of them."

I try to continue, being as controlled as I can. I remember what my psychiatric nurse told me before I confronted my parents with what I am about to tell my brother. "You're doing this for yourself," she told me.

I muster my energy to go on—I have been waiting for this for too long.

"You weren't very nice to me when we were young," I hear myself say. And as soon as the words have been spoken I realize that the distance I have put between us is equal only to the intimacy of what transpired growing up together.

"You're brilliant—look at the schools you went to," is my brother's disjointed response.

I forge ahead, repeating to my brother all the details I have been able thus far to remember, as well as how what happened has led me to where I am today.

When I tell him what I remember about my father, my brother begins to recount violent behavior I do not recall. "He would hit me with the end of the metal shoehorn," my brother tells me.

When I once again confront Jeffrey with what he has done there is a short pause before he says, "That's what kids do to each other. What is it that you want me to say?"

"I was hoping you'd be able to say you were sorry," I answer.

❧

More frightening than remembering is not being able to remember. That night I cannot get to sleep. My mind and heart race as I try to remember the last time I saw my brother—that unreachable scene at the edge of my memory enrages me more and more as each detail is recalled.

Who knows what arouses memory? Being once again in a familiar place? Seeing a face that reminds you of someone you have not seen in years? The repetition of a word or phrase heard long ago? The touch of your lover's fingers on your skin? Perfect quiet?

As I fall asleep I sense my brother. He is somewhere in the room near me. With my eyes closed I see him standing before the bed. My body shakes when I realize he is not wearing any clothes.

I try to take a deep breath when I see my clothes strewn on the floor and know I, too, am naked. I am a month away from seventeen. We are not in my college dorm—nor in his—but in the Lansman's bungalow the summer before I go off to college.

In memory it is difficult to discern how sex happens. Who first wanted whom? Who plays the seduced? The seducer? These shameful questions, and so many others, prevent me from remembering all that happened that afternoon in my parents' bed.

Tonight, as I fall asleep in my parents' upstate house, ten miles from the bungalow where what I am trying not to remember as I remember it occurred, I know that somehow, long after I was a helpless child, when I was old enough to know what I was doing, my brother is standing next to my parents' bed. My face is too close to his naked groin.

But what I remember next happened long after. Or did it? We are in my brother's Chevy. I am yelling at him through my tears when he forces me out of the moving car. As he drives away I yell at him long after I know he can no longer hear me.

❧

"Did you sleep okay?" my mother asks the next morning.

"Not bad," I say, knowing it was the pill I took that helped me sleep through the night. "Where's Jeffrey?"

"His friend's plane comes in this morning. He had to leave early," she tells me. Did Jeffrey tell them about yesterday's conversation?

"I heard the phone ring late," I say.

My father looks at my mother. "Nanny is in the hospital," she tells me on her way back into the kitchen.

"She needs emergency open-heart surgery," my mother tells me. "They thought she was fine but she . . ." She does not finish what she has started to say.

"Stupid woman," my father says as he gets up from the table. "She went from doctor to doctor until she found one who told her what she wanted to hear."

"What are you going to do?" I ask my mother.

"They'll call me if . . . ," again trailing off before she has been able to say what she wants to say.

As I eat my bagel my father's words, *stupid woman*, repeat in my head. Fifteen years ago, my maternal grandmother kept a tumor in her breast a secret for over a year. When she finally told my grandfather she had something important to tell him he thought after forty years of marriage she wanted a divorce. Soon after, she had a radical mastectomy.

I must have finished my bagel because my mother is already removing the plate, a habit she learned from her mother, who would hover by the table and remove the plates as soon as you were finished eating.

"Up so late," my grandmother would squawk the April she

was visiting us in 1977, the month I had graduated early from high school. Everywhere we went she would have a complaint: my aunt Bea's chicken salad was too dry, the waiter's armpit smelled, I stayed home doing nothing all day.

A week into her visit I had enough and refused to ride next to her in the car on the way to a cousin's bar mitzvah. "I'd rather not go than have to sit next to her," I announced before we were supposed to leave.

"That's the way you raise your son to talk about his grandmother," my grandmother carped at my mother when I made my feelings known. "He sleeps and does nothing all day long," she said as I started to leave the room.

No sooner than I had left the room, I was surprised to hear my mother tell my grandmother: "This is his house and he can do what he wants. And I do not want to hear you tell me how I have raised my son. I am very proud of the way I raised him and you are a guest here."

It could have been worse; he could have been a girl. The words my mother used to say. But it was a girl that my mother wanted, and never had. *It could have been worse; he could have been brain-damaged.* Other words I now remember. And my unspoken response long ago: Would that have been worse?

I find myself in the kitchen with my mother and I ask her: "Will you have to go?"

"I don't know. What can I do there?" my mother says, forcing a smile. "I'll decide after you leave."

I once again realize how important having the family together on this Thanksgiving has been for her. Through the running water I hear my mother's voice echo from years ago. I hear what she said when I found roaches in my bed: "I don't care who you sleep with, but I don't want you sleeping with roaches." And when I talk about what it might be like to have artificial legs: "You'd have to remember not to leave them at someone's house if you stay overnight."

As I watch my mother busy herself in the kitchen I hear what she said that late autumn afternoon when I was a graduate student at Columbia. Just before five o'clock, when it gets dark early, I picked up the phone and after saying hello heard her voice, in a lower register than usual.

"I'm in the house all alone," she said.

What was she trying to tell me? There was nothing unusual about her being in the house by herself in the hours between her coming home from work and my father's later return. What made my mother pick up the phone and call me that afternoon?

Over the years my mother and I have not agreed on many important issues, have been very angry with each other, have gone through many difficult times. Still, she has stuck by me in every crisis I have encountered. *I'm in the house all alone.*

Every night I was alone in the hospital what kept me going was knowing what my mother would bring with her the next day: Nathan's crinkle-cut french fries. As my mother continues to busy herself in the kitchen, I think about her standing outside in the unsafe neighborhood of Coney Island at ten o'clock in the morning, waiting for Nathan's to open so she could bring to the hospital what her son had asked for.

I'm in the house all alone. I go to her and put my arm around her, rest my head on her shoulder.

Later that night, I stretch out on the couch and my father eases the pain in his bad back by lying on the floor. I am surprised when my mother passes by the rocking chair and comes to join me on the couch. I lift my legs so she has enough room to sit down. When she does I do not know what to do with my raised legs. She pulls my feet down to rest on her lap, the first time I feel my mother touching my legs.

∾

In the pizzeria we sit in a booth in front of the just-out-of-the-oven pie. "Your mother's at the laundry, putting the clothes in the dryer. She'll meet us here," my father tells me.

Today, this has been my craving. I take a large slice, douse it with parmesan.

"Is your brother gay?" my father asks me. I almost choke on my pizza.

Since Helen told me five years ago, I have known that my brother is gay. She also told me that Jeffrey did not believe I was gay even after he read my first published poems.

"How am I supposed to know?" I answer.

"Do you think he is?"

Because I did not hear it from my brother, I convinced myself I can tell my father what I know without breaking a trust.

"Yes, I do," I answer.

I am on to my second slice when my mother, carrying a basketful of now dry laundry, enters the pizzeria.

"Come here, Joan," my father calls to her. "Do you know Jeffrey is gay?"

"I figured," my mother says nonchalantly as she sits at the table, placing the basketful of clothes next to her.

"Then why hasn't he told us?" my father asks.

I cannot believe this conversation is actually taking place in a Catskills pizzeria. I eat my third slice.

When nobody has answered him my father moves on to ask me if my brother knows that I'm gay. "It would be difficult not to," I say. "Can I have the last slice?"

I contemplate the fact that both my brother and I are gay. To my parents it means they will not have grandchildren, something that severely disappoints my mother, even though she has never spoken about it.

Was it because of my disability that my parents so readily accepted my homosexuality? Was it my disability, making their need for my brother to be what society could name as *normal*, that caused them to ignore and not honor my brother's sexuality? I know my disability has some place in this familial equation, but as with so many other aspects of my life, it is difficult to discern what effect my being disabled has actually had.

Sitting in the pizzeria in New York's Catskill Mountains, I think how little I know about my brother. His being gay has not brought us closer. Have we missed the opportunity to understand the family that we share? Have his relationships with men been affected by the violence as mine have? What has he remembered all these years?

∾

The noise stops and the table I am on moves forward out of the wall. I am helped back into the wheelchair and pushed through the now more active halls. In the elevator the light is too bright. I close my eyes.

I am returned to my psych-ward room, where it is still early morning and breakfast has not yet arrived. Sitting on my bed I stare out the window at the building that is my only view. I try to calm myself, remind myself I am no longer in the MRI tube, and bring myself back from what I have just remembered.

But my body will have none of it. I feel chilled, and when I cross my arms, palms to shoulders, to warm myself, my right hand instinctively finds the scar from the smallpox vaccination I was given on the upper part of my left arm after I was born. As my finger presses into my skin my body jolts—just like it did when taking the MRI.

As I look at that place on my arm I remember it. Or some of it. I don't know how old I am. I know my mother is at a sisterhood meeting at the synagogue. My father is a few steps away from me, bending over to check the roast my mother has left for us in the oven. I do not know where Jeffrey is but I know I am angry at him. I do not know what I say about my brother, but whatever I say angers my father.

After so many years, it is still one quick motion that propels my father toward me. Holding the metal fork—a moment before, he was checking my mother's roast—he burns my arm.

The sudden sensation lifts me off the stool on which I was sitting.

"Why did you do that?" I want to ask my father.

"You. You and your brother," he says before I am able to say one word.

For a brief moment, a moment as brief as it took him to burn my arm, my father and I are looking at each other.

When I turn to escape from the kitchen, my father is once again bending over, checking the roast with the same fork with which he burned my arm. Instead of walking past him, still short enough, I bend slightly beneath the counter that divides the kitchen from the dining room, go into the bathroom, and pour cold water on my arm.

Years later, standing in my hospital room, I still cannot remember what I said that caused my father to burn my arm. Even though I now know that whatever I said, I did not deserve to be burned, my not knowing what provoked such a violent reaction from my father—as if knowing what I said could explain my father's rage—disturbs me as much as the fact of his burning me.

As I hear the hospital hall enlivened by the delivery of the breakfast trays, my hand still protects my upper arm. When I remove my hand from my arm I see that I have inadvertently scratched the skin near the scar from the smallpox vaccination.

Having been startled awake too early, I am tired. Though I have spent the predawn hours horizontal while taking the MRI, it feels as if I have been run over by a truck. Looking out of my hospital-room window, I can only imagine what other surprises await me during the days ahead, as my body remembers, releasing the trauma that has been so long encoded in my skin, hidden deep in my bones.

❧

When I return home from Thanksgiving weekend, my mother flies down to Florida to see her mother. After heart surgery, on my parents' thirty-fifth wedding anniversary, my mother's mother dies.

When my father calls to tell me, I try to remember one good thing about my maternal grandmother. But all I remember is how my brother and I would go into her walk-in closet and rearrange her perfectly ordered shoes. One morning she had to call in sick for work because she could not find a matching pair. A good thing I cannot remember.

"How is Mom feeling?" I ask my father.

"She manages," he answers.

❧

Having phone sex is a way I can control what a man knows about my body.

On the phone-sex line I talk with a married lawyer. With his wife upstairs, we talk sex on the phone every night after midnight for two weeks.

"I think I'm falling in love with you," the married man tells me. I quickly turn the conversation back to sex.

When I tell my psychologist the married man is coming to Provincetown for a visit I also tell him I have yet to tell my phone-sex partner I am disabled. "I never lied," I assure my psychologist. "I just dodge the height question."

"You neglected to tell me something, haven't you?" the married man says as he sits down in my living room.

"I figured you'd find out when you got here," I offer. "Otherwise you probably wouldn't have come."

"I'm so confused," he tells me. "I've been married for over ten years. I have two children and another on the way. Despite your problem you seem so sure of who you are."

My *problem*? Instead of sex, the married man takes me out for dinner. He shows me photos of his wife and kids.

The next day the married man calls me from his office to tell me how angry he is. "You lied to me. You set me up," the married man says. "You should have told me about your legs." I do not have a response so I wait to see what else he will say. After a long silence he continues. "You were right. If you told me about your legs I wouldn't have come." There is another silence. Does he actually expect me to apologize? Finally, he realizes I still have nothing to say, and during the silence he hangs up.

A call from the phone company goes a long way toward convincing me my foray into phone sex has gotten out of hand.

"Mr. Fries?" the woman's voice mispronounces my name, using the long *i* so my name sounds like a side order at Burger King. "I'm from New England Telephone and we wanted to let you know that your phone bill this month has exceeded four hundred dollars, and since this amount is much greater than your usual bill we thought you might like to know." As she speaks I think that the woman from New England Telephone's voice sounds far happier than it should sound.

"While I have you on the phone, Mr. Fries"—once again mispronouncing my name—"there is a considerable amount of toll calls to 900 numbers and we wanted to make sure you know we now have available a service that blocks these toll calls if there is someone in your home who you do not want to be able to make these calls." Is she reading off a cue sheet? "Perhaps you have young children in the home—"

I interrupt her and satisfy her that I am aware of the calls, and thank her for letting me know how large my bill is going to be. "Is there anything else I can do for you today, Mr. Fries?" Again using the long *i* since I neglected to correct her after her first two mispronunciations.

"No, that about does it," I say.

That week, I inadvertently mention to my psychologist how large my phone bill is going to be. When I do so, he tells me he does not think he should be taking a fee much lower than his usual rate if I am able to spend so much on phone sex. Without further discussion, I agree that it would be best that I not make any more phone-sex calls.

I tell him about Charlie, the first man with whom I had sex when I moved to San Francisco. Years ago, when I returned from Israel I surprised myself by asking Charlie what he felt about having sex with a disabled man. "I concentrate on the good parts," is what Charlie told me, also answering my unstated question of why during sex he never touched my legs.

"How did you feel when he said that?"

"I thought he was great to be so honest."

"That wasn't my question."

"I felt as if a whole part of me had been erased." I take a deep breath. "I don't think it's good for me to have any kind of sex with someone if I can't be honest about being disabled."

~

I am at a residency near Chicago, finishing *Anesthesia*, a book of poems, when Myra, another writer in residence, tells me: "You must meet my friend Kevin."

How many times have I felt that I will never be able to make love again? This feeling is prevalent the year after I begin to live alone. Can I now trust enough to be intimate with a man? Will I be too afraid to fall in love again?

I am first introduced to Kevin, a painter, at the international art fair on a cold Chicago day. He takes us over to the gallery where his work is showing. His work, arm gestures and their mirrored reflections, intrigues me. When we part, he gives me his card.

Later that week, Myra arranges for us, and another friend, to have dinner with Kevin. That night, I discover he is well read; he discovers I can talk about art.

During dinner I go to the bathroom. Returning to the table, I notice that Kevin is staring intently at something or someone behind me.

"What are you staring at?" I ask him.

"At the couple who are staring at you."

"It happens all the time," I hear myself say as I sit down. "Kids always ask me why my legs are the way they are."

"What do you tell them?" he asks, once again looking at me.

"I tell them I stayed too long in a hot tub."

We both burst out in uncontrollable laughter.

"What are you boys laughing about?" Myra wants to know, but every time Kevin or I try to tell her, our laughter gets in the way.

After dinner, we go back to Kevin's apartment and convince Myra to take out her tarot deck. "You've met someone who will turn out to be very important to you," she tells Kevin as she reads his cards.

Later that week I call Kevin, and he invites me to Chicago. "I'd like to show you the Art Institute," he tells me. "Will you be able to get around?"

"If I take it slow, I'll be okay," I say.

When I meet Kevin in Chicago, we spend the entire day at the museum, go out for dinner, and by the time we stop talking it is well past midnight.

"You can stay at my place," Kevin tells me.

Kevin has only one large bed, but when he hands me a pair of pajamas I do not know what is on his mind. All night, even though I want to touch him, I do not want to be rejected. Does Kevin feel the same?

The next day, we drive to where I've been staying and spend the day in Myra's studio. "Read us some poems," she says.

The thought of reading the poems about disability that I've been writing, all those scars and bones, in front of Kevin makes me anxious. I do not want to make myself vulnerable.

"I'd like to hear them," Kevin says.

Very reluctantly, I read them some poems. It is worse than being naked, I think, and the familiar feeling of everyone's eyes being on my legs returns.

After dinner Kevin is supposed to take the train back to Chicago. "He can stay longer if you'll drive him," Myra says.

"I don't want to drive back and forth so late," I say.

"You can stay at my place again," Kevin says. I see Myra look at me. She didn't know I had spent last night at Kevin's. "But nothing happened," I want to tell her.

That night, back at Kevin's, we do not wear pajamas.

"I had a nervous breakdown last year," I hear myself tell him. "It's been like learning to walk again. Not the first time—that I can't remember—but like after surgery when I was ten, when I refused to let my reconstructed right leg touch the floor. I was so afraid it would no longer be able to bear the weight of my body."

Extended on top of his naked body, I relax all my muscles, putting the entire weight of my body onto his. Every touch, like every observation when I first returned home from the hospital, is magnified. I am no longer standing in the shallow end of the pool.

∾

Ten days later I return to Provincetown. Before leaving Chicago, I told Kevin I wanted him to visit, but not for just a week, when we would have to spend the entire time catching up. Three weeks later, Kevin calls to tell me he wants to come spend the summer with me.

That summer, our relationship is romantic but without the underlying desperation. Our lovemaking is both passionate and playful. I feel no need to measure, as if there were a way to do so, if my attraction to his body is greater than his attraction to mine. When I wake up in the middle of the night, moving closer to him, I do not feel my body insignificant or incomplete. In the morning, I know Kevin will not wake up hungover. I trust he will not be quickly desiring another man.

More importantly, I do not hesitate to tell Kevin all of my story. When old feelings are stirred up, even when I am not sure he will understand, I at least tell him what is going on. When we disagree or have an argument it does not feel like our relationship is imminently going to end.

"When did you want me?" I hear myself ask Kevin at the end of the summer.

"When you read your poems," he tells me.

ॐ

Until now, my paternal grandmother, ninety-six, except for cataracts, is healthy. Then, surrounded by her great-grandchildren at my uncle's house, where she has been living, she has a stroke that leaves her in a coma.

Every night, after driving the hour-and-fifteen-minute commute from work in New Jersey, my father drives an extra hour to see his mother, unaware in a hospital bed. Every night he sits by his mother's side, pouring water on her dry lips, squeezing her hand, wanting to let her know that he is with her.

"Every night, riding up in the hospital elevator," my father tells me, "I imagine that when I get to her floor, I open her door and see her sitting up in bed, happy to see me."

My father imagines this for three weeks. Then she dies.

From old photographs and papers my father finds among what my grandmother has left behind, I learn more about where my family came from. But most of my unanswered questions about my family's origins remain unanswered.

When Anna Fries died, with her went my family's last link to the Eastern European shtetl culture of the nineteenth century. It wasn't anything my grandmother imparted that stays with me; it is the image of her drying her laundry on the fire escape in the middle of winter that I remember.

My paternal grandmother learned a way to make things work for her, and tried as hard as she could to keep it that way. Only when she grew too old, only when she was forced by circumstances out of her control, did she allow herself, and then only reluctantly, to depend on others. Her stubbornly proud refusal to change her often anachronistic ways is what remains. I often think that, somehow, this trait skipped generations and is my inheritance from her.

Two months later, Kevin and I are writing and painting in New Mexico when my parents come to visit. After five days of traveling around, we stand next to the rental car. Saying goodbye that morning in Santa Fe, my father begins to cry.

"I haven't been the same ever since Grandma died," he tells me. "I had a good time seeing you here where you're so happy. Let me see you again. And Kevin. Soon."

From the car my parents wave. As they pull away, I feel as if I am once again their child in the hospital, and even though they left my bedside only moments before, I am already anxiously waiting for the next day when they will return. And although I am standing with Kevin under the vast expanse of the New Mexico sky, when I can no longer see their car, somewhere I hear the hospital elevator close, the sound that begins to stir the distinct loneliness I still carry with me after all these years.

∾

"Most of my patients who tell me how perfect their child-hood was turn out to have been abused," Dr. Riskin tells me.

It seems that I have lived much of the past fifteen years trying to tangibly reconcile what I could not piece together as a child. Do my unsuccessful attempts prove that such reconciliation can only be forged in memory?

I want to ask the psychiatrist: How, in memory, to reconcile the distinctly contrasting images of my father. How to integrate the contradictory actions of my mother. Is there room to include the gift of that still unidentified toy in the portrait of my brother, who beat me up and threw me out of his moving car?

I sort through these images as if making a scrapbook of old photographs newly found. I select parts of different photographs, assemble parts of each into a collage, building a picture of each member of my family so I can plainly see before me my father, one hand bathing my feet; his other hand burning my arm.

And my mother sits on hall patrol in front of my kindergarten class door; yet on the other side of the door is the broken furniture and the phone that has been ripped from the wall, the remnants of the violence she does not protect me from, that she chooses to ignore.

And in the center, I am surrounded by a circus of dissonant images, my younger self staring not at my father, not at my mother, not at my brother. I stare at none of them. I look directly at my present self as if demanding to know what I should by now know—the answers to the questions in that child's eyes.

Closing the book I have created in my mind, I wonder when, if ever, I will be able to hold all these images of my family

steady in my vision without having to turn away from them—
or without having to constantly juggle each part of each separate image from grasping hand to grasping hand. The question
remains: How to learn to hold on to the entirety of this cacoph-
onous constellation—all at the same time—in what once was a
child's hand.

❧

Kevin decides that one in his next set of paintings will be
about my shoes. I ask if he can just use my shoes, made from a
plaster mold, one built up three inches to compensate for the
height differential between my legs, like Van Gogh used them.
But after he tells me it is important that I am pictured wearing
my shoes, I agree to let him take photos of me and my shoes,
which he will use as the source for his painting.

After Kevin sets up the room with extra lighting, he asks me
to lie on my back, to lift my legs, to hold them in the air. When
I do so, he begins to take his pictures.

As I keep my legs dangling in the air, I am laughing. But
soon my laughter ends and in the silent room an embarrassment I have not felt for a long time resurfaces, overtakes me. It
is as if I am once again walking down a city street, followed by
youngsters who yell after me: "Why are your shoes so big? Why
do you walk that way? Why are your legs the way they are?"

Then I am once again being passed from stranger's hand
to stranger's hand. All attention is on my legs. I begin to
sweat, breathing becomes difficult, a heavy haze descends over
my eyes.

When I try to speak to Kevin I do not have any words. It is as
if I am an infant who does not yet have the ability to speak.
When I try to once again say something I quickly stop myself,
afraid that what will emanate from my mouth will be unintelligible sounds.

During a lull in the shoot, I curl up in a ball on the bed, and when Kevin has decided what he next wants me to do, I cannot move.

"What's going on?" Kevin says as he joins me on the bed.

Not wanting him to see me this way I hide my head under a pillow. I want to disappear.

Kevin, attempting to calm my fears, is explaining what his painting of my shoes will be about. *Demythologizing difference.* I can barely hear what he says. *The perception of beauty.* Right next to me he sounds as if he is miles away.

"Look at me," he says.

I bury my head further under the pillow.

"You wanted to model for me for the longest time," he tells me.

Slowly, I remove a hand from the pillow and without looking at him I reach out to touch him. When I touch his arm I feel his hand move over mine.

From beneath the pillow I peek out at Kevin, but when I do I see he is looking at me. His gaze moves right through me, sending that all too familiar feeling rushing up my spine. I can only look at him for a brief moment before I must once again avert my eyes.

"Take your time," he tells me. I realize his hand is still on mine.

It is as if my body has been drained of all energy. My stomach is as if inside out; it seems I will not be able to eat for days. All the signs point to the beginnings of being in the grips of another depression from which I am powerless to escape. Under the pillow, I breathe deep, trying to slow things down.

First, you'll feel good for one minute a day, I hear the nurse's voice tell me, *then the next day, you'll feel good for a minute and a half.*

Another deep breath, and finally I am able to briefly look at Kevin. I am, after one more aborted try, able to remove the pillow from my head.

Still curled up I crawl over and rest my head in his lap. Kevin begins to run his hand slowly through my hair.

"I want to paint you like that golden Buddha," he tells me, reminding me of the photo on the cover of the guidebook I bought when I started planning a trip to Thailand six months ago.

"I'm sorry," I say. "I didn't know this would happen. I thought after all this time I had a handle on all this. It's very frustrating that no matter how hard I try it never actually goes away."

∾

At the end of the first floor of the permanent exhibition at the National Holocaust Memorial Museum in Washington, D.C., the history of the Nazi persecution of the physically and developmentally disabled is displayed. After an entire floor devoted to the Nazi rise to power and their ruthless treatment of political opponents, Jews, Gypsies, and homosexuals, the first group to be systematically annihilated by the Nazis—the disabled—briefly becomes the focus of the exhibit.

Beds from the hospitals, and equipment used to conduct medical experiments on and eventually to dispense with the disabled, accompany the wall text, which tells about the laws used to legalize such mistreatment. The text tells about T-4, the code name for the project at the notorious killing center, the hospital at Hartheim. At the end of the first floor, I am the only visibly disabled person in front of the exhibit, reading how Zyklon gas was first used to kill the disabled, years before it was used to exterminate the Jews.

I imagine I am trapped in these beds behind the partition. Visitors gaze at me with horror and pity. What they see, a helpless child strapped to a bed, stirs up emotions they would rather not feel. Some stay a long time and wide-eyed, stare. Others quickly escape across the glass-enclosed bridge to the museum's other side. How similar their reactions are to those whose stares and fears I have met on the streets of many places in countries all over the world.

Only after I leave the museum, by reading books I find in the library, do I learn that many of the ideas used by the Nazis were initially espoused by the eugenics movement in the first years of this century in the United States. Only then do I learn that the forcible sterilization of the developmentally disabled took root first in my own country and was still practiced only a short time before I was born.

Later that summer I attend "The Art of Memory: Holocaust Memorials in History," an exhibit at the Jewish Museum in New York City. As I slowly make my way through the exhibit, a docent-led group follows. Since I take an inordinate amount of time in museums, wanting to read all the labels, the group is about to overtake me halfway through the exhibit.

I have just passed the photographs of the two Holocaust memorials in Amsterdam when I decide to wait in order to let the group pass me by. While waiting, I hear what the docent tells her group, consisting of men and women of my parents' generation, men and women who would be comfortable at my parents' traditional Rosh Hashanah kiddush held annually in the living room of their Cropsey Avenue apartment in Brooklyn.

"Now, all of you know about Anne Frank, and this is a photograph of the Anne Frank House in Amsterdam. But not too many of you know what is pictured in the photograph we just passed," the docent is saying to these would-be friends of my parents. "Here, in Amsterdam, is the Homomonument. Built in 1987, it memorializes the Nazi persecution of homosexuals, who were also sent to concentration camps, where they were forced to wear the pink triangle. The triangle is the major element in the canalside design."

When the docent leads the group onward to the section of

Holocaust memorials in Israel, I let them pass me by. I sit and watch the video, tucked away in the corner, which documents the sounding of sirens that stops all activity in the streets of Israel during an annual moment of remembrance.

I am almost finished viewing the exhibition, in the section devoted to how the postmodern aesthetic has been used in building recent Holocaust memorials, when I realize in this exhibition I will see no monument built to remember those disabled persons who were killed by the Nazis. I will see no such documentation because such a monument has not yet been built.

Before I leave the museum I buy the exhibition catalogue and search it to make sure I have not overlooked this glaring omission. I read the section on the Homomonument, which tells me this "stunningly understated" memorial is just around the corner from the Anne Frank House, and that it "consists of a large marble triangle traced in the ground: one corner is raised, another flush with the surrounding cobblestones, and the third juts out slightly over the edge of the nearby canal." I learn that the Homomonument, placed at the center of the matrix of Amsterdam memorials, has each of its three axes pointing: one to the Anne Frank House, a second to the Amsterdam Gay Coalition offices, and the third to the National Monument.

When I have satisfied myself that no mention is made of any monument to the disabled, I go back to the passage on the Homomonument and read the section's conclusion: "This assures that present life is lived as a constant negotiation with the past."

Sitting in my friend Marcia's Upper West Side apartment I begin to conjure up my own Holocaust Memorial for the Disabled, and I think about the day the United States House of Representatives passed the Americans with Disabilities Act, remember the photograph on the front page of the *New York Times*.

When I get back to Provincetown, I take out a file where I have saved the clipped article. "House Approves Bill Establishing Broad Rights for Disabled People," the headline reads. And there in the photograph, among the bill's supporters who are, according to the photo caption, reacting at the Capitol to televised coverage of the debate, are Jean Stewart, the first disabled writer I met, and Marilyn Golden, my first disabled friend. Looking at the photo, which includes these women in their wheelchairs, smiling as they applaud, I know there is a limit to what you can achieve in isolation.

I find a front-page photo that I have not remembered. This photo does not have an article attached. It pictures a group of disabled activists crawling up the large terraced steps in front of the Supreme Court of the United States. The caption tells of the demonstration, which illustrates the inaccessibility that most disabled persons encounter in their daily lives. The demonstrators, the caption tells us, were arrested.

Two years later, these photographs are joined by another in my file. This new photograph, together with the accompanying article, again clipped from the *New York Times*, is about the controversy surrounding the approval of the proposal for the long-delayed monument to Franklin Delano Roosevelt that will be built in Washington, D.C. This monument, which will join the memorials to Abraham Lincoln and Thomas Jefferson on the Mall, will not depict FDR as the disabled person he was when he was elected president. "Roosevelt was very desirous of keeping his disability out of the limelight," Lawrence Halprin, the monument's designer, is quoted as saying. "Should a President who used a wheelchair be recalled in one?" a pull quote asks.

The accompanying photo shows FDR, in formal attire, standing with a hand linked through the upper arm of another formally attired man. In FDR's hand is a cane, barely noticeable because it blends with the dark suits both men wear. The caption for the photo reads: "A photograph from a dinner he attended while President shows how he tried to keep his disability out of sight; a body guard helped steady him."

Adjacent to the article there is another photograph. This photograph shows the on-site sign for the Franklin Delano Roosevelt Memorial, which illustrates the proposed design and includes a three-dimensional photograph of a smiling, stetson-wearing FDR, cropped to show nothing from the waist down.

I take my file and go into the living room to replay the videotape of the documentary on FDR that recently broadcast on public television. I fast-forward until I see the historian Hugh Gallagher is speaking. Gallagher, in view of his wheelchair, is talking about the tremendous drive that fueled FDR's quest for the presidency, years after his bout with polio. Gallagher tells the interviewer, "Disability is commonly viewed as either madness or inspiration."

Madness or inspiration. I rewind the video to hear these words again. *Madness or inspiration.* Rewinding, *madness*, replaying, *inspiration*, rewinding, replaying, until I have heard enough.

Before I close the file I take one last look at the photos I have saved: my two friends cheering the passage of the civil rights bill; the disability-rights activists crawling up the steps to the Supreme Court of the United States; the smiling FDR, cropped at the waist, next to the plan of the memorial that will be built to remember him; FDR, still smiling, being surreptitiously propped up by another man.

But another image floods my mind. This one comes from the Academy Awards show. When reciting the nominees for special effects, the presenter mentions how the filmmakers implanted Tom Hanks as the fictional Forrest Gump in actual newsreels depicting many former presidents. Then Gary Sinise is shown playing Forrest Gump's friend, a war veteran with amputated legs. The presenter tells us, and film clips illustrate, how, by having the actor wear a certain tone of blue pants, they were able to portray Sinise's character as having stumps for legs. By shooting Sinise in this way, on film his character's legs disappear.

The night of the Academy Awards I dream I am playing basketball like I did when I was a boy. Before I wake, the long legs I have in the dream disintegrate—disappear like Gary Sinise's do on film in *Forrest Gump*. But in the early morning, when I wake up to get a drink of water, it is just like Dr. Milgram promised my parents it would be. I am able to feel my own legs carry me across the cold floor from my bedroom into the kitchen.

℘

Dr. Riskin has me meet with her supervisor. With Dr. Riskin present we talk about what brought me to check myself into the hospital.

"He's quite glib," the supervisor says to Dr. Riskin, as if I am not present.

"Glib?" I want to say, but remain silent.

"I would recommend you not talk with him about the physical pain," he tells Dr. Riskin. "He will use that to not talk about what he actually needs to talk about."

Finally, Dr. Riskin's supervisor talks directly to me. "I want you to realize that your having experienced abuse has nothing to do with your being disabled."

"What?" This time I say what I want to say.

"I want you to realize that your having experienced abuse has nothing to do with your being disabled," he repeats.

"How could you say that?" I say, still not believing what I have just heard.

"There is nothing to prove you would not have had the same experiences if you were not disabled."

I could offer this doctor many valid reasons why his statement is not true, but realize that no matter what I say he will not change his mind.

"Glib?" I say to Dr. Riskin when she comes to see me in my room after the meeting with her supervisor is over.

"He didn't mean it the way you are taking it," she tells me.

"I've never before in my life been called glib."

"He means that you use words very well and that sometimes that hides what you must be feeling."

"I don't think I'd be here if I was trying to hide what I'm feeling," I tell her.

"I didn't agree with everything he said," Dr. Riskin admits.

"I would hope not. That stuff about the abuse having nothing whatsoever to do with my legs. That man has no understanding of what it is like to be disabled," I tell her.

"But your brother wasn't disabled and he was abused by your father," she asserts.

"The point is I've experienced my abuse that way—even if it's not the reason, and who can actually pinpoint the reason—somewhere deep inside me I think I was abused as punishment for all that I caused because I was born disabled.

"I know being disabled is only a partial answer," I continue. "There doesn't seem to be an answer that satisfies every question."

༄

When Matthew, back in the States and now a rabbi, calls to tell me he is using *The Healing Notebooks* as part of a sermon, I am surprised. Ten years after I met him in Israel, Matthew has yet to come to terms with his homosexuality.

"Your poems always seemed Jewish to me," he tells me.

"Jewish? That's the last way I'd imagine my poems would be described."

"You take nothing for granted. You're always asking questions," he explains.

Matthew tells me he is in the midst of a battle to make his synagogue accessible. "They don't understand it's not okay for my disabled congregants to have to use the back door," he complains.

"You're the only person I know who understands disability without my having had to teach it to you," I tell him.

"Meeting you was important," he says, contradicting the long silence between us. We have seen each other only twice during the past ten years. "And you sent me Marilyn." I had forgotten that I had Marilyn call Matthew when she visited Israel soon after I returned.

"How was I able to be myself with you back then?" he asks.

I want to tell Matthew to pay attention to what his body tells him. But when I was in Israel I was not only unsure about my body, I also did not know how to draw sustenance from my growing awareness of who I was. I have no suitable answer to Matthew's question.

"Just remember it happened," I tell him.

∾

When channel surfing on the television Kevin accidentally alights on a telethon. "Turn it off," I tell him.

"I hate telethons, too," he assures me.

As a child, besides Scott, the midget in my school, and some kids I met in the hospital, the only other disabled people I saw were on the telethons. Though I never watched the Jerry Lewis muscular dystrophy telethon, every year I watched the one for cerebral palsy. Except for sleeping, I watched it from beginning to end.

"Have Steve and Eydie come on yet?" my mother would ask as I remained glued to the television set, watching the amount pledged mount higher and higher toward the goal as the weekend progressed.

One year I asked my mother if I could pledge my month's allowance. I called up the number that kept flashing on the screen, and when my pledge envelope arrived the next week I felt very proud.

Around this time, in school, I first learned about Darwin's *The Origin of Species* and his theory of the survival of the fittest. As my teacher spoke I kept reaching down to touch my legs, as if to make sure they were still there. I began to feel that everyone in the room must be looking at me—with these legs I was not fit enough to survive.

Since living with Kevin, I've made sure I have house-keeping help other than my lover. But still the physical imbalance between us sometimes takes its toll. Most people who help the disabled do so in the hope of cure, or at least to alleviate a temporary physical situation. I'm afraid that when a disability is chronic not many will stick around for the long term.

I take the remote control and mute the TV. After three years of living together there is still so much I want to explain to Kevin. Outstretched on the couch, my legs in his lap, I ask him: "Do you realize my disability is, over time, not going to get better? It will remain the same or get worse as I get older. How I deal with it might change, but my body itself, there is no chance for improvement."

"I know that," Kevin tells me before turning his attention back to the television.

As he holds my feet in his lap, I realize my wanting to explain is caused as much by my insecurity as by my need for him to know. I want to believe what Kevin has told me is true.

It is late Friday afternoon and I am resting on my bed when Dr. Riskin comes into my room.

"Do you need to change our Monday morning appointment?" I ask.

Standing in front of the other bed, which during my first week in 2 East has remained empty, Dr. Riskin hesitates before answering.

"I've been debating whether or not to tell you this," she says, "but after getting to know you the past week, I think you'd want to know." She pauses again.

Then she looks directly at me. "Before my residency here I worked with children who were ill and had to spend a lot of time in the hospital. Like you did," she tells me. "I wanted you to know that today things for these kids are different from when you were young. In the hospital I worked they set up cots in the rooms, allowed the parents to stay overnight. Before surgery, the staff would demonstrate what procedures would be done to the child by using dolls. They encouraged the kids to keep the dolls after the surgery was over.

"I debated whether or not to tell you what I know because I realize that it might make you very sad that you were not able to get such attention when you went through what you did. But I also know that when this episode in your life is past, you care enough that you would want to know that things can be different for kids who are born or become disabled today.

"Oh, the MRI shows nothing abnormal in your back. You're scheduled to meet with biofeedback after I see you on Monday. Perhaps that will help you get a fix on what you can do to alleviate the chronic pain. I'll see you Monday morning."

When she is finished she leaves me sitting on the edge of my bed, still looking at where, just a moment before, she stood. As

I stare at the empty bed across from me I think: By luck of the draw I'm given the psychiatry resident who understands the piece of my past that no other professional has known firsthand before.

∾

Ten years ago, if told that my old friend Helen would need to go into an addiction treatment center to withdraw from drugs, I would not have been too surprised. But if asked if I would have knowledge of recovery, of healing, to help my friend whom I so admired when growing up, I would have had to answer no.

Six years ago, if told that Jason, who never altered his self-destructive behavior, would until recently remain healthy, my response would have been more than skeptical.

Only a few years ago, if told that I would have as friends a group of disabled activists and writers I would have been filled with disbelief. If told that after relationships with Jason and Miguel I would meet Kevin, that after my disability progressed to the point where I could no longer take for granted what I once so easily did on my own, that after a nervous breakdown that led me into the hospital—after all this—I would find myself still uneasy, but more fulfilled, I would have laughed myself out of the room.

Growing into awareness, I have learned the price of letting go—the shedding of beliefs, images of myself, friends, all of which I once thought were necessary sustenance, things I could not live without. Now, through grief and sadness, I try to pay attention to what matters, which as I grow older becomes easier to discern.

Tonight, when I call Kevin into the bathroom, I do not want him to kneel beside the tub. I do not want to rest my feet in his palms as he washes my feet and legs. I want him to take off his clothes and join me, naked. I want to place my soapy feet on his chest and begin to explore his body. I do not want to close my eyes and merge by memory what I feel being with him in the tub with what I could not feel many years ago. Tonight, I want my sense of time to be different. When he touches me I want to keep my eyes open.

But at times, especially at night when I am trying to fall asleep, it is still difficult for me to be intimate with my lover. Since the panic attacks began, I am afraid that having sex before I go to sleep will cause them to happen all over again. And even though when before sleep nothing much has transpired, more often than not I will wake up three or four hours after I have gone to bed. I will wake up with my heart racing, and despite all that I now know, and even though so many years have passed, it is still as if what happened to my body then is still happening now.

Tonight, lying next to Kevin, I try to visualize the radiation that I know must still flow through my body. When I first learned that X rays could cause sterility, I tried to remember every X ray that had ever been taken of my body—as if by being able to know the exact amount of radiation to which my body had been exposed, the side effects would not occur.

I still want to know why when Kevin touches me, experiences in which he has had no part are somehow reactivated and I am still like that child who years ago lay powerless under the X ray's eye, still plagued—now both of us—by what we cannot see.

What if I told Kevin that after years of living together I still fear that our relationship will turn out to be just another version of what happened with my brother? That when he is angry I am afraid that he will burn my arm?

What if I told him that my history with men causes me to doubt my judgment, so, despite anything he might do, I will doubt my choosing him, too? I want him to know that long after my previous relationships are over I am still haunted by those men. That when I drive down familiar streets in cities where I know Miguel no longer lives, I think I see him again. I think I see him again and a moment later I realize the man I thought was Miguel looks nothing like him, nothing at all.

Does Kevin understand how all this relates to what has happened? How much of it do I understand? Is memory simply a selective replaying of the past, a justification of how you need to think past events have happened? Can anyone comprehend how the mind reacts to what the body remembers?

Is it true that once you are forced against your will to experience something your body is supposed to enjoy, you remember those experiences over and over until they become part of every situation that involves being touched by someone you love?

What if I told Kevin that even though I know what happened years ago is not my fault, I still feel responsible that it happened? How do I tell him that even though I know I am not responsible for being born with deformed legs—I gave that up years ago, didn't I?—I feel responsible for how my disability causes me problems now? That no matter how many times he tells me how attractive I am, so much within me, as well as so much that surrounds me, conspires to tell me otherwise? How can I make him understand that although remembering is necessary for acceptance, forgiveness takes a much longer time?

I watch my parents slowly getting older. Their memory, containing so much of my history, is beginning to dim. When they can no longer remember there will be nobody to ask my unanswerable questions. When they are gone I will once again be left alone with my brother. By that time will I have forgiven him?

I get up and turn on a light in the living room. Outstretched on the couch I look at my legs. With my fingers I trace the familiar scars.

Tonight, I notice changes. Changes I have not noticed before: the two small toes on my right foot more curled; the angle from which my right foot juts out from my leg more extreme; the bone near what would be my left ankle pushes further through the skin; my left heel further to the side.

I run my hand under that part of the sole of my right foot that never touches the ground, compare the smooth skin there with the calluses on the left side of my right foot, the side I now walk on. How much longer until my foot will be twisted all the way around and I will be walking on the top of my foot? How long can I postpone surgery? How much longer will I be able to even walk on these legs that have gotten me around for over thirty-five years?

Tonight, I cannot stop looking at my legs. I think by looking at my legs ever so carefully, with just the right amount of attention, I can begin to notice the imperceptible changes that are now just beginning, the changes that will eventually cause my feet to look like—*what*? I try to imagine what my legs will look like ten years from now. Something even the best orthopedic doctor could not tell me: What will be the difference in time?

Looking at my legs I still do not know when I first learned to walk. My parents still have not been able to tell me. I think about my parents, miles away, sleeping in the same apartment they have slept in since three months after I was born. I wonder how long it has been since they last dreamed the shoemaker's store, where they still bring my shoes to repair, is on fire. I wonder if knowing I now have an extra pair protects them from having this dream.

I try to re-create the scene my parents have yet to tell me, the scene in which I learn to walk. Why do they not remember? I no longer believe I learned to walk while wearing two casts. I want to know if I was able to walk because of Dr. Milgram. I want to know if I was able to walk because of my mother's headstrong perseverance. How much do I owe my walking to my own stubborn determination? Or was I walking toward my father's beaming eyes?

I no longer live near water. In the middle of the night I still hear the traffic from the highway, sounds others claim not to hear. But now the sounds of these passing cars come from farther away. Here, there are no sirens.

I get back into bed with Kevin. The streetlights throw shadows on the walls.

No matter where I go, children still stare at me in the street. Some follow me; others are afraid. And like that boy who waited for me on the stoop every day on my way home from school, some still ask me the same question. How do I tell them that some questions have no answer?

ACKNOWLEDGMENTS

The author would like to thank the PEN Writers Fund and the Authors League Fund for financial support; the Djerassi Resident Artist Program, the MacDowell Colony, the Ragdale Foundation, Villa Montalvo, and the Virginia Center for the Creative Arts, for residencies that provided the time and care needed to write this book.

Grateful acknowledgment is made to Helene Aylon for initial listening; Jocelyn Lieu for early reading; Monica Wood for procedural suggestions; and Sue Standing for the Swahili proverb.

The support, knowledge, and perspectives of others who live with disabilities have added much to this book: Gene Chelberg, who listened to countless passages over the phone; Victoria Ann-Lewis, Katinka Neuhof, and Susan Nussbaum, who have been blessings; and Marilyn Golden, who has been for many years the right person at the right time. I am proud to call these leading writers and minds of the disability-rights movement my friends.

Thanks cannot do justice to the generous and wise editorial insight of Sarah Schulman, whose honesty and wisdom illuminated the first draft of this book; and Anne Finger, fellow traveler, writer, and friend, whose perceptive reading of the second draft pushed me even further.

Much appreciation to Jed Mattes for his belief in my work even before this book entered anyone's mind; Fred Morris for more than attending to my numerous phone calls; Kevin Bentley, with whom the idea for this book originated; Alex Swenson for considerate attention; and Carole DeSanti for having the forethought to publish this, and for her brilliant, sensitive editing.

This book could not have been written without Chuck Madansky, who guided me through the years when I remembered; my parents, brave as they are; and most of all, Kevin Wolff, who put up with my extended absences, emotional and physical, while this book was written—our relationship grew as the book did.

FASCINATING MEMOIRS

☐ **AMERICAN ELEGY** *A Family Memoir* **by Jeffrey Simpson.** The unforgettable portrait of an America, a way of life, and a family that are vanishing even while coming to indelible life on these haunting, exquisitely written pages. Simpson, the last of his line, fluidly moves across the hopes and struggles of many generations, exploring the transformation of the people of a once vibrant culture into the ghosts of the past. (941223—$23.95)

☐ **TWO OR THREE THINGS I KNOW FOR SURE by Dorothy Allison.** Allison turns from fiction to memoir, weaving the story of her own family's history in rural South Carolina into a meditation on the meaning of storytelling. She tells the story of the Gibson women—sisters, cousins, daughters, and aunts—and the men who loved them and often abused them. "Dorothy Allison is, without question, one of the finest writers of her generation."—*Boston Globe* (273404—$8.95)

☐ **VERTIGO** *A Memoir* **by Louise DeSalvo.** In 1958, DeSalvo saw Alfred Hitchcock's *Vertigo* eleven times in one week. Transfixed by the lead character's fainting spells (which she too suffered) and by the image of woman-as-imposter falling to her death, the film seemed to embody all the confusing messages she was receiving as a young woman. In her memoir, DeSalvo vividly recounts her attempts to transcend the limits of her working-class girlhood and forge an identity based on her own desires. A brilliant example of a woman writing her life in a manner that defies conventional wisdom and refuses to suppress the truth. (273242—$11.95)

☐ **A MOTHER'S STORY by Gloria Vanderbilt.** Carter was handsome, brilliant, on his way to a successful career and on the mend from a broken romance when at the age of twenty-two he committed suicide before his mother's eyes. Now Gloria Vanderbilt tells the story of his life and death, and the story of her life and her struggle to live on after that death, in the most moving book a mother has ever written about her son—and the most honest and revealing book a woman has ever written about herself. (278228—$10.95)

☐ **A WHOLE NEW LIFE** *An Illness and a Healing* **by Reynolds Price.** In 1984, Reynolds Price, one of America's most notable writers, learned he had cancer—a ten-inch-long, eel-like tumor inside his spinal cord that seemed certain to kill him. Now, in this fiercely honest account of a refusal to die and a quest for a way to live, he tells the story of his agonizing illness and extraordinary cure. (274737—$11.95)

Prices slightly higher in Canada.

Visa and Mastercard holders can order Plume, Meridian, and Dutton books by calling
1-800-253-6476.
They are also available at your local bookstore. Allow 4-6 weeks for delivery.
This offer is subject to change without notice.